Employment Relations in Aotearoa New Zealand

Employment Relations in Aotearoa New Zealand

An Introduction

ERLING RASMUSSEN; FELICITY LAMM; AND JULIENNE MOLINEAUX

ER PUBLISHING
AUCKLAND

Published by ER Publishing

Contact: erbooksnz@gmail.com

A catalogue record for this book is available from the National Library of New Zealand.

ISBN 978-0-473-63250-2 (paperback)
ISBN 978-0-473-63251-9 (EPUB)
ISBN 978-0-473-63252-6 (PDF)

DISCLAIMER

This publication is developed and distributed on the terms and understanding that:

- The authors are not responsible for the results of any actions taken on the basis of information in this publication, nor for any error or omission from the publications, and
- The publisher is not engaged in rendering legal, accounting, professional or other advice or services.

The publisher and authors expressly disclaim all and any liability and responsibility to any person, whether a purchaser or reader of this publication or not, in respect of anything, and of the consequences of anything, done or omitted to be done by any such person in reliance, whether whole or partially, upon the whole or any part of the contents of this publication.

Contents

Preface

Employment relations is part of our daily life and is often featured in political debates and media reports. It is not surprising therefore that many employers, unions, academics and ordinary people take a personal interest in employment relations and how their employment relationships develop over time.

The book is concise and concentrates on key areas, trends and themes. It is intended to be a practical introduction and guide to employment relations issues as well as an introduction to the principal legislative changes. It also provides the reader with recent sources of information for future reference.

In recent years, New Zealanders have witnessed major reforms that in turn have resulted in significant changes in employment relations. While the fundamental relationships between the government, employers and employees still remain, there have been changes in how these parties interact as well as changes in the associated employment outcomes. These changes will also affect how we work and will be working in the future. Technological innovations, globalisation and a different workforce composition have facilitated innovations in work practices and in employment patterns and this book tries to bring these influences to the fore of our discussion of employment relations.

Erling Rasmussen, Felicity Lamm and Julienne Molineaux

March 2022

1. Introduction and overview of employment relations

ERLING RASMUSSEN; FELICITY LAMM; AND JULIENNE MOLINEAUX

1. To define employment relations and describe how it operates across all levels of business and a range of disciplines
2. To identify the major participants in employment relations
3. To show how the balance between collective and individual employment agreements and rights has changed over time
4. To examine the core principle and content of employment agreements, including the distinction between employees and contractors
5. To highlight how the roles of the Employment Institutions and legal precedent have influenced the practical application of employment relations changes

Introduction

Most of us are either employed in paid or unpaid work, or employ people ourselves and, therefore, have some understanding of what employment means. Employment relations are often described as the interaction between three major groups: employers, employees, and the government. But it is more than this; employment relations are dynamic and complex and what occurs in the workplace is influenced by the wider society. Governments change employment laws from time to time, and courts interpret these laws when they rule on cases. This creates precedents – new understandings about the application of law, which essentially become new laws.

Rapid technological change has resulted in both a change in the type of jobs available, and the way that work is done. The 'future of work' has become a catch cry and is often associated with very positive or negative predictions about job opportunities or disappearance of jobs (see discussion in Chapter 6). Some of these changes are already detectable. Thus, the 'standard employment relationship' – an assumption that work is full time, stable, with set hours and unionised – is no longer the case for most New Zealanders. Many people work part time or long hours and job and income insecurity appear on the rise. Technology is disrupting boundaries between work and leisure, something that has become pronounced after the Covid-19 pandemic in 2020. Businesses often want the flexibility of longer operating hours and variable staff rosters and can use contracting models to better control wage and salary costs. Thus, many people work as contractors and contracting has become dominant in certain industries and occupations. Recently, contractors have started to provide services administered by various web-based platforms as part of the 'gig economy'.

Overall, there are many influences beyond the local and national labour markets. Workers in New Zealand compete in globalised job markets as firms outsource production to countries with lower labour costs. Furthermore, government policies facilitate immigration and emigration, allowing the New Zealand workforce and its skill and education makeup to change faster than it would without international labour mobility.

This chapter defines 'employment relations', the different levels of employment relations and it examines the key 'actors' who influence employment relations. The chapter also overviews the basic elements of an employment agreement and will in subsequent chapters deal with historical and current changes to the employment agreement itself and to its key components such as pay, hours, leave and dispute resolution. The chapter will also highlight the distinction between employees and contractors and why this distinction came to be of great importance. Finally, we focus on employment institutions which deals with disagreements over employment agreements and disputes in workplaces. As there has been rapid change to employment relations – including an expansion of employee rights and less collective bargaining coverage – there has been considerable focus on court-based employment decisions.

Finally, there are major disagreements about core employment relations issues and how to interpret the above-mentioned changes and influences. How we view employment relations is contentious as we each have our own outlook (or perspective) based on our individual set of beliefs and values (as discussed in Chapter 2). Often, we tend to align ourselves with those who share our views and the various perspectives can be found in disagreements between the key parties in employment relations as well as political decisions on legislative frameworks and employee rights (see Chapters 3, 4 and 5).

What are employment relations?

The definition of employment relations has broadened over time and is still evolving. The subject of employment relations has developed an interdisciplinary approach using concepts and ideas derived from several disciplines, including sociology, economics, psychology, history and political science (see Chapter 2). Our current definition incorporates conceptual elements from both UK industrial relations and USA labour relations as well as from human resource management theory. The issue of collective disputes between workers and employers has dominated traditional definitions of employment relations, with a fixation on conflict between employers, unions and employees. As shown below, there have been considerable changes recently as employment relations has superseded the traditional concepts of industrial or labour relations and their pre-occupation with collective bargaining and industrial disputes.

Power

Power is an important aspect of employment relations. Power refers to the ability to influence the behaviour of others to get what you want. In an employment relations context, power is important *within* organisations as different actors have different levels of power in that organisation. Does a low-paid employee have the same level of power when discussing workplace issues as the manager or business owner? How do these power differentials impact on relationships and outcomes? Additionally, power in the *wider society* is also important because different groups and interests – including government, employer groups and unions – try to negotiate policy outcomes that favour their own group or interests and reflect their values and priorities.

Traditionally, industrial/labour relations were concerned with 'macro' questions, including how employers and businesses are a part of the wider community and how they play an important role in society. In particular, industrial/labour relations have focused on three aspects of the employment relationship, namely: the key parties (employees, employers, and government), the processes of collective bargaining (including conflict resolution), and the outcomes of these processes (Bamber et al., 2016). In particular, the way collective conflict was regulated has received plenty of attention. Regulating industrial conflict involves the development of formal rules – such as written employment contracts and policies – and of informal rules – such as custom and practice (see Chapters 13 and 14 in Rasmussen, 2022). Thus, the focus is on structures that regulate matters of conflict arising out of the employment relationships which includes the regulation of power relationships in the workplace. Additionally, industrial/labour relations have traditionally concentrated on unionised, male, manual workers employed in large factories and have tended to ignore workers in service industries, workers in small workplaces and non-unionised employees.

The rise of Human Resource Management (HRM) since the 1980s has also had a major influence on our understanding of employment relationships. HRM emphasises a strategic approach to achieving organisational goals and involves a series of management prescriptions designed to ensure the efficiency and commitment of employees (Boxall & Purcell, 2011). The focus of HRM is, therefore, on the individual organisation and the way the individual worker can be managed in order to enhance the achievement of broader organisational objectives. As a result, HRM has been linked closely with motivation in the form of psychological and economic dependency. The emphasis is on winning the 'hearts and minds' of the workforce in order to achieve the common goals of the organisation (Bratton & Gold, 2017; McAndrew et al., 2018).

The traditional views of both industrial/labour relations and HRM have been challenged while, at the same time, extracting the more useful aspects from the two disciplines. As a result, the distinctions between industrial/labour relations and HRM have become blurred, creating an over-arching discipline called 'employment relations' (Bamber et al., 2016; Kelly, 2012). This shift in definition has the advantage that it extends the boundaries of industrial/labour relations and HRM to include all aspects of the two approaches. Most important of all, it has incorporated both the 'macro' or broader approach adopted by industrial/labour relations and the 'micro' or organisational approach of HRM. It is recognised, therefore, that the employment relationship does not exist in isolation and can be found on many levels: international, national, industry, organisational and workplace levels.

Levels of employment relations

What occurs in New Zealand employment relations is often influenced by *international* trends and events. International trade agreements, the operations of multinationals and the pressure to conform to international labour conventions and treaties all have an impact on the way employment relations are conducted in this country. For example, multinational companies' movement in and out of a country typically depend upon whether or not that country's labour and compliance costs will benefit the multinational organisation financially. Concern has been expressed in New Zealand about the way multinationals influence our wages and conditions by choosing to set up their manufacturing operations in nearby poorer countries with weaker employment protection legislation, in direct competition with New Zealand manufacturers. Employment relations at a national level are also influenced by international institutions, such as the International Labour Organization (ILO), of which New Zealand was a founding member. Since its foundation in 1919, the ILO has been involved in the promotion of international labour standards (see https://www.ilo.org/global/lang–en/index.htm). In recent years, the ILO has become more important through promotion of Decent Work principles (see Ferraro et al., 2015) which have also influenced legislative changes and public policy discussions in New Zealand.

Most decisions regarding New Zealand employment standards are taken at a *national* level. Employment standards are contained in national statutes that govern how people are employed, their minimum level of pay, and their conditions of work. For example, the Human Rights Act 1993 establishes anti-discrimination standards; the Minimum Wages Protection Act 1983 sets standards for minimum wages, and the Health and Safety at Work Act 2015 provides guidelines for health and safety in the workplace (see Chapter 5). Economic, social and welfare policies constructed by government also have major consequences for both employers and employees throughout New Zealand. For example, the government policy decision to deregulate the automotive industry in the late 1980s and to reduce tariffs resulted in the closure of car manufacturing plants and other related businesses. Likewise, the changes to immigration rules during the Covid-19 pandemic had major labour market repercussions and created recruitment problems in several industries.

Although there is a national framework of employment relations standards (see Chapters 4 and 5), general parameters for wages and conditions are, more often than not, set at the *industry* level. For example, a qualified motor mechanic with three years' experience will have a good idea of how much they should be paid by making relative comparisons with other mechanics who have the same level of qualification and experience. Wages and conditions within industries can be set either directly or more indirectly through flow-on effects. Wage rates and specific conditions can also be negotiated directly between the representatives of employers and employees at an industry level (see the discussion of Fair Pay Agreements in Chapter 4). In the last three decades, there has been a shift from collective, industry-based wages and conditions to workplace-based, individual employment agreements (see Chapters 3 and 4). This has created a much wider divergence in pay and conditions; not only between industries but also between occupations, workplaces and individual jobs within particular organisations.

Corporate decisions can have either positive or detrimental effects on an organisation's employment relations. Strategic decisions, such as the introduction of new technology, the way the company is structured, the opening or closing of new plants and offices, or the introduction of new management practices, will affect the lives of the organisation's employees. Decisions taken at the corporate level about redundancies, less job security, etc., are also likely to have a detrimental effect on the workforce. However, some employers have purposely adopted human resource policies and implemented corporate strategies that will enhance their employment relations as well as their public image. But as organisations change over time, so do their strategies. For example, in the past New Zealand-owned companies have had strategies that fostered harmonious employment relations and longer term commitment to their company (see Chapter 6). But as the companies changed ownership and senior managers left, new managerial strategies were implemented to reflect the new ethos of the organisation. It is at this level, too, that HRM strategies – such as good communication and innovative reward systems – are most effective in motivating the workforce and improving employee morale and satisfaction.

However, it is at the *workplace* level that the employment relationship is most keenly felt. The day-to-day activities and how they are managed will often determine the quality of the relationship between supervisors and staff. For example, as a result of the replacement of complex organisational hierarchies with team-based organisational structures, some employees can have a large degree of autonomy over how they work. This influences aspects, such as the allocation of tasks, the design of the job, the allocation of overtime, and so on. The move toward team-based structures has also produced a change in titles – the terms 'supervisor' and 'staff' have been replaced with 'team leader' and 'team members' – but the question is: has it changed hierarchical divisions? The devolvement of responsibilities to the workplace level in the last decades has had a significant impact not only on how we work but also on our employment relationships in general. Likewise, greater employment flexibility and atypical employment arrangements have also impacted on employment relationships and this is, in part, why there is such a debate about the potential influences from various 'future of work' scenarios.

Employment relations can be studied, therefore, at the international, national, industry, corporate and workplace levels, and can be affected by external factors, such as technological change, market conditions, societal and political power shifts. It is clear, therefore, that the nature of employment relations can only be fully understood in the context of, and in relation to, wider socio-economic, political and legal structures.

Interest groups

The subject of employment relations is also concerned with the study of how individuals, groups or organisations desire their interests to be represented (collectively or individually), and what these interests are; for example, the amount of pay, hours worked, or production output. Interest groups are organised groups of people – who are not political parties – who come together to influence laws and policies.

As mentioned above, employment relations laws and policies are not created in a vacuum. There are many competing interest groups who aim to influence how employment regulations are enacted and implemented. Indeed, some argue that national decisions concerning the creation of employment regulations are essentially a compromise between the wishes of powerful interest groups and those of the government (see CIPD, 2017). According to this view, the government is to be regarded as serving primarily the interests of those whom it regulates, namely the employers and employees. At the corporate level, employers and employees are in competition with one another for power and control over the decision-making process, knowledge, information and technology, though more power and control normally rest with management.

The government

Historically, the government has played a central role in New Zealand's employment relations, although the nature of its activity has varied from direct, centralised government control to a more hands-off approach whereby markets are left to organise employment relations with less state intervention. Irrespective of the extent of government involvement in employment relations, it is a critical player, creating the framework within which employers and employees interact. This framework influences the balance of power between employer and employee interest groups and provides structures for conflict resolution. This relationship is bound by conventions developed over the last century with the government establishing an employment relations framework through legislation and legal institutions (see Chapter 3).

Government departments have the responsibility for regulating and promoting compliance with the raft of employment legislation that deals with issues like working conditions and minimum wages (for example, through the Labour Inspectorate in the Ministry of Business, Innovation and Employment [MBIE]). During the 19th century, concerns about the working conditions of women and children, as documented in the 1890 Sweating Commission, led to the establishment of a system of statutory minimum conditions contained in the Factories Act 1891 and later the Industrial and Conciliation Act 1894.

Subsequently throughout the 20th century, legislation was updated with some Acts being amended and others replaced. Like Australia, New Zealand had adopted an award system. Under the award system, different award documents contained occupation- and industry-specific minimum wages and conditions, including, the level of pay, hours of work, special rates for overtime, dangerous or piece work, etc. However, the system ceased with the enactment of the Employment Contracts Act 1991 and, as a consequence, employment relations statutes, such as the Minimum Wage Act and the Holidays Act, have become more important as they now provide the minimum standards.

The current legislative framework, the Employment Relations Act (ERA) 2000, therefore, is supported by other legislation that sits alongside and stipulates, for example, adult and youth minimum wage rates, paid annual leave requirements and personal grievance and disputes procedures. The statutory minimum standards contained in these supportive employment relations statutes are regulated by MBIE's Labour Inspectorate while employment or 'personal' grievances are enforced through the Employment Institutions. Personal grievances and employee rights are discussed later this chapter.

New Zealand employment laws and procedures are also formed and defined by the country's legal system. Under the ERA 2000, employment matters are handled by the MBIE's Employment Mediation Services, the Employment Relations Authority and Employment Court. The government continues to separate out employment matters from other legal issues as a way of ensuring that it retains a role in the regulation of employment relationships and that employees have direct access to procedures which allow them to seek redress for employer actions (McAndrew, 2010; Rasmussen & Greenwood, 2014).

However, periodically, there has been pressure both inside and outside the New Zealand Parliament to abolish specialist employment law institutions (Rasmussen, 2009, pp. 83-84). The desire to discontinue a separate employment legal system was based, to a large extent, on the employers' criticism of the Employment Court's decisions. In particular, such criticism was levelled at the Court's firm intention to uphold the notion of 'procedural fairness', its recognition of and accessibility to employee representatives, its opposition to harsh and oppressive contracts, and its views on home workers' contractual status (Anderson & Hughes, 2014; Simpkin, 2006).

It should also be remembered that the government is, itself, not only a regulator and arbitrator, but also a substantial employer. Many of its employees work in essential service areas such as policing, defence, health, education and welfare. The government is also an indirect employer through its procurement practices (Ravenswood & Kaine, 2015). Many New Zealanders are employed in either privately-owned companies or non-governmental agencies that receive substantial funding from the government. People working in both private and public sectors are covered by the ERA 2000 but public servants are also covered by the State Sector Act 1988. The latter Act follows public sector legal tradition by making provision for a separate negotiating body, the State Services Commission.

Since 1988, the employment practices of the public sector have fallen more in line with those of the private sector. Chief executives of government departments now have the freedom to employ, dismiss, promote and discipline staff – with the exception of senior executives. Most government departments have expert employment relations advisers to ensure good practices and that the departments meet the requirement of being a 'good employer' as set out in the State Sector Act.

Employers

There are many groups that represent a range of employers' interests. For example, there are Chambers of Commerce, industry and trade associations, and employer groups such as Business New Zealand that specialise in employment matters. In the 1980s and 1990s, employer lobby groups placed increasing pressure on the Labour and National governments to enact radical labour market reforms. At the heart of their argument for labour market reforms was the notion that the traditional protection of trade unions and centralised collective bargaining was, in fact, diminishing the rights of both employers and employees, undermining business competitiveness and creating unemployment (Harbridge, 1993).

One of the more effective employer lobby groups in New Zealand was the Business Roundtable (NZBRT). Founded in 1985, membership of the Roundtable was by invitation only and restricted to the chief executives of New Zealand's largest companies. The NZBRT promoted a consistent view of employment relations, in line with 'right-wing' or libertarian ideology (Harris & Twiname, 1998; Kelsey, 1997). This included vocal support to end compulsory trade union membership and promotion of more individualised employment relations. The NZBRT had considerable influence on public policy during the 1985-1996 period. However, it lost the ear of governments from the late 1990s onwards. In 2012, they merged with the New Zealand Institute to form a new think-tank, The New Zealand Initiative.

However, far more representative of employers' interests are the employers' and manufacturers' associations situated in the main regions. Business New Zealand was created after a merger of the Employers' Federation and the Manufacturer's Federation in 2001, and has specialist divisions for representing, at a national level, the interests of exporters, manufacturers, and its Major Companies Group. The employers' and manufacturers' associations also provide a range of services – from training to legal representation – for their members. However, like the trade unions, they have had to adjust to the deregulated economy and rapidly changing employment environment of the last decades.

The other significant representative of employers' interests is the Chambers of Commerce. Established over 160 years ago the branches are also located in the main New Zealand regions. Like the employers' and manufacturers' associations, they offer a range of employment relations/HRM services. Finally, there are business groups that have been formed to respond to a particular issue, for example, the Business Leaders' Health and Safety Forum. Launched in 2010, the Forum is a coalition of business and government leaders representing about 300 private and public sector organisations with the aim of improving the performance of workplace health and safety in New Zealand.

Trade unions

Trade unions have represented the interests of New Zealand employees in one form or another since the 19th century. Their role was supported and aided by earlier government legislation which ensured compulsory union membership and access to disputes procedures. However, the Employment Contracts Act 1991 abolished the unions' monopoly position as an employee interest group. As a result, there was an immediate decline in trade union membership. The loss of members was precipitated by the move to individual employment contracts, by disaffected members leaving the unions and by frequent job shifts by employees. From May 1991 to December 1999, union membership fell by more than 50% to 302 405, and union density (the number of union members as a percentage of the workforce) declined from 41.5% to 17.0%, although the number of trade unions stayed roughly the same (see Chapter 3).

This decline severely weakened the power base of the two major employee associations that represent a consortium of trade unions, namely the Trade Union Federation (TUF) and the Council of Trade Unions (CTU). The Council of Trade Unions (CTU) was the larger of the two and, in 2000, represented 21 affiliated trade unions and more than 240 000 employees. By 2001, a merger of the CTU and TUF had brought state and private-sector unions under a single umbrella grouping. Mergers of unions have continued and, in 2016, the CTU represented 31 unions and more than 320 000 employees.

However, trade unions had already started to consolidate their position at the end of the 1990s and, with the introduction of the ERA 2000, they have managed to stabilise their membership numbers, though with private sector unions facing an uphill battle (see Tables 3.1 and 4.1). In addition, there have been a number of mergers creating 'super unions'. For example, in 1996, the Engineers Union merged with the remnant of the Communication and Energy Workers Union and the Print, Packaging and Media Union. This created the largest private-sector union, the New Zealand Amalgamated Engineering, Printing and Manufacturing Union (EPMU), with nearly 60 000 members. In 2015, EPMU further merged, with the Service and Food Workers' Union, to create E tū. In 2011, the FIRST Union was created through an amalgamation of the National Distribution Union (organising primarily workers in the transport and warehousing industries) and Finsec (organising workers in the bank and finance industries). Finally, the Public Service Association (PSA) has sustained a strong presence in the public sector as has other public sector unions, such as the teachers' unions, the nurses' union and the doctors' unions.

There have also been new union organising strategies, of which the Living Wage Campaign is one noteworthy example. The Living Wage Campaign is a response to the phenomena of working poor, in which working full-time on a minimum wage is not enough to meet living costs, but also is not enough to live with dignity and to be an active citizen in New Zealand communities (Carr et al., 2018). By approaching and working with community groups including churches, the Service and Food Workers' Union (now part of E tū) campaign had, by 2016, managed to get about 60 accredited employers to pay 19.80 NZD per hour (compared with the minimum wage of 15.25 NZD per hour.)

In summary, the interests of the three main groups can be represented on a continuum. At one end are the employers who want to ensure that they are not unreasonably impeded from managing their businesses and making profits. At the other end are the employees who desire fair wages and conditions and some say in the way they work. The government lies somewhere in between these two groups, providing a buffer for the employees and attempting to control the extremes of the employers. In reality, however, the employers' and employees' representatives do not restrict themselves just to workplace matters but endeavour to influence government policies on a wide range of issues – from paying fire service levies to social welfare and benefit payments.

Employee versus contractor?

Another key feature of employment relations is the distinction between *contracts **of** service* and *contracts **for** service*. This distinction has evolved over centuries and has been carried through to the current legislative framework. Contracts *of* service or employment contracts cover employees working for wages or salaries; that is, employees in factories, shops, offices or professional occupations. Contracts *for* services cover self-employed contractors, who work for others under contract to provide distinct jobs or services. This involves tradespeople, taxi-drivers and many professionals such as lawyers and doctors. That is, the contractor may do the same tasks as an employee, but their legal status is different from that of an employee: contractors are not covered by the employment relations legislative framework in New Zealand. Contractors are, therefore, not entitled to receive the so-called 'minimum code' of statutory protections, such as holidays and other types of paid leave, minimum wages or equal pay. Certain implied terms that are present in every New Zealand employment agreement by statute or common law are not present in ordinary contracts for service (Lamare et al., 2014).

With new forms of jobs and individualised employment and working arrangements, more and more employment situations have arisen where it is difficult to distinguish between employees and contractors. This is often the result of new organisational strategies (in particular, the search for labour flexibility), attempts to reduce income taxation or attempts to avoid the statutory employee protection stipulated by the ERA 2000 and its associated Acts. Determining whether a worker is a contractor or an employee can also be difficult but there are some basic distinctions, as presented in Table 1.1.

Table 1.1 Key features of employment contracts and contracts for services

	Employment contracts	Contracts *for* services
Control and management	employer has right to control and manage work	contractor controls and manages work
Integration	the worker is 'part and parcel' of the organisation (e.g. wears uniforms)	contractor may take work from other 'principals'
Hours of work	set by employer	contractor may work hours of own choice, provided work gets done
Tools and equipment	provided by employer	provided by contractor
Form of payment	linked to time worked (hourly, weekly, etc.) and with wages paid on a regular basis	contractor paid for job as a whole
Profit and loss	borne primarily by employer	contractor is in business on own account
Payment of sick pay, holiday pay, PAYE etc.	responsibility of employer	responsibility of contractor
Service	employee must give personal service	contractors may send someone else – including their own staff

Sources: Rasmussen & Lamm, 2002, p. 55; Lamare et al., 2014

Different courts have also decided whether a worker is a contractor or an employee, but the rulings can be conflicting. For example, in the New Zealand case *Bryson v Three Foot Six Ltd.* (2003, 2005), the Employment Relations Authority decided Mr. Bryson was a contractor but the Employment Court and the Supreme Court decided Mr. Bryson was an employee (see the Special Issue of the *New Zealand Journal of Employment Relations*, 2011, 36(3), for a more detailed discussion of these decisions and the so-called 'Hobbit' legislation in 2010).

Notwithstanding the different legal decisions, the courts have developed a number of tests over the years in order to establish whether a person is working under an employment contract or under a contract for services (Anderson & Hughes, 2014). There are basically four such tests:

- the control test
- the organisation test
- the business test
- the composite test (involving all of the previous three tests).

These tests are important because they indicate key characteristics of an employment relationship. The control test, for example, indicates that the employment relationship is a power and authority relationship. This authority is often referred to as 'managerial prerogative' – that is, the ability to manage other people and to issue demands. However, some employees can have a significant amount of discretion in how they do their work and as a result the control aspects become less clear-cut. This is the case, for example, with many highly skilled employees such as computer specialists, academics, legal or financial specialists.

This discretion is important in the organisation test which asks whether the employee is part of an organisation or whether the work the employee does is central to the organisation. The business test attempts to establish whether the person is running a business or whether the person is dependent on an organisation. Finally, the composite test is an assessment of the employment status that takes the three previous tests into account. This test is probably the way that court decisions are moving as the distinction between being an employee or a self-employed contractor becomes more and more blurred. However, in particular cases, the court will place greater emphasis on one or another of the tests, as appropriate.

In summary, while contractors retain rights and protections under general contract law, these rights, however, do not equate to those defined by employment laws designed to protect employees from what the ERA 2000 calls 'the inherent inequality of bargaining power in employment relationships'. In the next section, we will explore employee rights, employee agreements and institutions in more detail.

Employee rights and the Employment Institutions

Under the conciliation and arbitrations system (1894-1990), the legislative framework had a focus on collective bargaining and collective agreements while individual agreements were dealt with under common law. This meant that many employees had no access to pursue employee rights through the Employment Institutions. This changed with the ECA 1991 where *all* employees had an employment contract/agreement and their employee rights could be pursued through the Employment Institutions (see Chapter 3). This is still the case under the ERA 2000, though this Act uses the term employment agreements (and so will this book) and is more prescriptive about the types of agreements allowed and their content.

Generally, employment agreements are made up of different components. The key components of an employment agreement are:

- the agreement itself (whether verbal or written)
- statutory entitlements
- customs and practice
- implied terms.

The employment agreement often consists of more than one

document. It could include a separate job description or the so-called 'House Rules'. The House Rules specify the workplace culture and particular ways of behaving in the workplace and can also provide detailed information regarding aspects such as use of equipment, company cars and the corporate wardrobe.

The agreement has to be in keeping with the statutory entitlements of employees, which are currently prescribed partly in the ERA 2000 and partly in a number of other Acts relating to industry, workplace and work practices (see, for example, the discussion of occupational health and safety in chapter 5). Customs and practice relate to workplace practices that, over time, have become a norm and that both employers and employees take for granted. For example, some workplaces may close early for Christmas or the organisation may be closed for the whole of Anzac Day. While such norms are important in creating a positive workplace culture and in running the day-to-day affairs of an organisation, problems can arise because of a lack of clarity and because they do not provide clear guidelines in respect of accountability.

Implied terms are norms that have become accepted as minima through many years of legal precedent. They concern certain basic rights and obligations with which employers and employees will have to comply. These include employee obligations such as turning up for work, following the employer's directions, and looking after the organisation's property and other employees' well-being. On the employer's side, it includes obligations to provide a safe workplace, to deal honestly with employees and to pay them the agreed wages. Thus, the rights and obligations often relate to behaviour that most people would regard as a matter of common sense (for more detail see Anderson & Hughes, 2014).

What could an employee expect to find in an employment agreement? The content of such agreements varies according to the job, the organisational culture and existing contractual arrangements. While some employees have a verbal employment agreement, most employers and employees prefer a written agreement as this clarifies the rights and obligations of the two parties. A written employment agreement has been prescribed as the norm under the ERA 2000 (see Chapter 4). Presented below are a number of items that are often found in employment agreements. The absence of some of these items from an employment agreement may have important implications.

Employment agreements are governed by statutory entitlements, customs and practice, and implied terms. This means that there are certain entitlements which cannot be undercut by any employment agreement. The statutory entitlements are mentioned in the ERA 2000 (see Chapter 4). There are, for example, existing default personal grievance procedures that will come into play if no such procedures are specifically included in an agreement. Likewise, there are minimum leave entitlements and statutory minimum wages both for adult and youth workers. Finally, inherent in the implied terms is that the employment agreement can cover only legal arrangements. Thus, in respect of employment, civil and criminal law, the agreement must not include any unlawful stipulations.

This means that such unlawful conditions or conditions below statutory minimum conditions, even if agreed to in an agreement, cannot be upheld. In other words, even if an employer and an employee have agreed on a wage below the statutory minimum wage, it would nonetheless be possible for the employee to seek a back payment from the employer, equal to the difference between the agreed and the statutory minimum wage for the period of employment. Thus, having an employment agreement provides significant protection and this makes the distinction between an employee and a contractor/self-employed person very important.

Table 1.2 Employment contracts and standard employment conditions

Terms of the contract	• starting date • position and duties • variation of contract • house rules
Hours of work	• standard working hours • overtime • breaks (tea or meal breaks)
Leave provisions	• annual leave • public holidays • sick leave • parental leave
Remuneration	• salary or wages? • wages and salaries: payment period and review period • wages and salaries: performance pay or bonuses • wages: penal rates and overtime pay
Employment terms	• termination • redundancy • retirement
Grievances and disputes	• codes of conduct • misconduct and dismissal • procedures: personal grievances and disputes
Other provisions	• occupational safety and health: prevention, procedures and reporting • new technology: planning, implementation and training • company information and confidentiality • training: availability, link to remuneration and promotion

Source: Rasmussen & Lamm, 2002, p. 54

Employment institutions and personal grievances

The establishment of specific Employment Institutions became a major feature of New Zealand employment relations with the introduction of the Conciliation and Arbitration Act 1894, and they are still a major feature under the ERA 2000. Unsurprisingly, the names, roles and specific functions of the Employment Institutions have changed considerably over time. The current Employment Institutions are the Mediation Service, the Employment Authority and the Employment Court and their roles and functions are discussed in Chapter 4. The personal grievance has been a crucial employee right since the Employment Contracts Act 1991 extended access to the personal grievance procedure to all employees. Since then, legislation has afforded employees the opportunity to decide themselves whether they would lodge a personal grievance claim, whereas previously, the claims procedure had been conducted through unions. This led, as was expected, to a rise in personal grievance claims (see Chapter 3). Since the mid-1990s, the Employment Institutions have had to deal with several thousand cases a year and most of these cases are personal grievance cases.

The personal grievance right has been controversial and it has often generated very critical employer evaluations (Walker & Hamilton, 2011). Some employer associations have pointed to some employees developing an 'American litigation' mind-set, especially when some employee representatives have an outcome-based fee structure whereby the employee only paid the representative if the case was won. The employee has, therefore, little financial risk in pursuing a personal grievance claim (Burton, 2004; 2010).

Another frequent employer complaint has been the emphasis on procedural fairness by the Employment Institutions (see below). Such employer advocacy has been criticised as exaggerating the lopsidedness and levels of payments associated with the personal grievance right, and instead personal grievance is seen as a useful constraint on the employer prerogative and promoting better conflict management (McAndrew, 2010). However, the 2008–2017 National-led Governments abolished the automatic personal grievance right of new employees – it was now up for negotiation (the so-called 90-day trial period) – which have influenced employment norms amongst young and low-paid employees (see Table 2 in Foster & Rasmussen, 2017, p. 102). While the post 2017 Labour-led Government has reversed several of the 2008–2017 changes, it is noticeable that it has kept the 90-day trial period for organisations with less than 20 staff.

Most of the personal grievance claims concerned unjustifiable dismissals. This probably suggests that a better understanding of the dismissal procedures by employees and employers alike was necessary. There are three types of dismissals (Anderson & Hughes, 2014, pp. 359-370):

- the standard, general type of dismissal
- summary dismissals
- constructive dismissals.

We will concentrate on the standard, general type of dismissal and only briefly describe the two other types. *Summary dismissals* occur when the employee is dismissed instantly and without any notice. This is a very drastic action that should only occur very rarely and only when the employee is guilty of serious misbehaviour. What constitutes 'serious misbehaviour' will alter over time but the term is normally associated with stealing, fighting, deliberately disobeying the employer's requests, and with a disregard for other persons' safety and health. *Constructive dismissals* occur in situations where the employee feels under pressure to resign. This can include situations in which a manager has 'leaned' heavily on an employee through constant criticism, allocating inconvenient rosters, or through publicly expressed dissatisfaction with the work performance. It can also include a situation in which the employee is given the choice of resigning or being dismissed.

A dismissal is only justifiable if it is fair and reasonable. This implies that there must be adequate *justification* (due cause) and a *fair process*.

Adequate justification would include misconduct, dishonesty or lack of punctuality on the part of the employee. However, dismissals are often associated with so-called 'performance problems', where the performance of the employee has fallen short of the expectations or standards set by the employer. In the case of performance problems, the following elements are important: the expected standards must be clear and the employee must be aware of the standards; these standards may not have suddenly changed, and the employee must have received adequate training and supervision to meet the expected standards.

Under the Employment Contracts Act 1991, the idea of a fair process, also known as *procedural fairness*, received a lot of attention (Anderson & Hughes, 2014, pp. 344-359). Key elements of a fair process are a *discussion* of the issues at stake between employer and employee and *issue clarity*. These key elements are important as each party should understand the other's position and also what changes and outcomes are sought. Procedural fairness includes giving the employee the opportunity to rectify the problem and making sure the employee understands that he/she could be dismissed if the problem is not solved. The employee should, in other words, be aware of exactly what the problem is and should know what to do in order to rectify it. The employee should also be given adequate time to rectify the problem and a clear warning must be issued that his/her employment could be terminated if the problem is not rectified.

If the warnings do not bring about the changes sought, then it may be necessary for an employer to consider terminating the employment relationship. In such situations, procedural fairness is important and Fryer and Oldfield (1994, p. 71) have recommended the following steps:

- 'give a proper explanation to the worker of the reasons that dismissal is being considered, including details of alleged wrongdoing;
- give the worker the opportunity to put their side of the story – defenses, explanations, any mitigating factors;

- make a full investigation of the situation before coming to a final decision. This includes taking into account the worker's explanation, interviewing other staff members where necessary, etc.'

Despite these relatively simple guidelines, many employers have complained about the complexity surrounding personal grievances and how decisions in the Employment Institutions can negatively influence employing and managing people. While these are controversial and contested positions, the changes in employment regulations have featured strongly in political debates (see Rasmussen, 2009, pp. 11-15).

A particular problem has been the crucial importance of legal precedent – that is, court decisions on key legal issues – in formulating precise guidelines for bargaining and workplace behaviours (Caisley, 2004). This can be a long-winded process and it can lead to shifting legal interpretations which can be difficult to understand for the average employer and employee. While the ERA 2000 has tried to limit the importance of legal precedent by having a prescriptive legal framework, there are continuously new challenges to the precise interpretation of legislative principles and their practical application (Greenwood, 2016).

References

Anderson, G. & Hughes, J. (2014). *Employment Law in New Zealand.* LexisNexis.

Bamber, G.J., Lansbury, R.D., Wailes, N. & Wright, C.F. (2016). *International & Comparative Employment Relations.* Sage.

Boxall, P. & Purcell, J. (2011). *Strategy and Human Resource Management.* Palgrave Macmillan.

Bratton, J., & Gold, J. (2017). *Human resource management: theory and practice*. Palgrave Macmillan.

Burton, B. (2004). The Employment Relations Act according to Business New Zealand. In E. Rasmussen (Ed.). *Employment Relationships. New Zealand's Employment Relations Act* (pp. 134-144). Auckland University Press.

Burton, B. (2010). Employment relations 2000-2008: an employer view. In E. Rasmussen (Ed.). *Employment Relationships: Workers, Unions and Employers in New Zealand* (pp. 94-115). Auckland University Press.

Caisley, A. (2004). The law moves in mysterious ways. In E. Rasmussen (Ed). *Employment Relationships. New Zealand's Employment Relations Act* (pp. 59-76). Auckland University Press.

Carr, S., Parker, J., Arrowsmith, J., Yao, C. & Harr, J. (2018). The Living Wage in New Zealand and its Implications for Human Resource Management and Employment Relations. In J. Parker & M. Baird, M (Eds.). *Big Issues in Employment* (pp. 95-108). CCH New Zealand.

Chartered Institute of Personnel and Development (CIPD). (2017) *Power dynamics in work and employment relationships: the capacity for employee influence* (Research report Part 1 – Thematic literature review). https://www.cipd.co.uk/Images/power-dynamics-in-work-and-employment-relationships_2017-the-capacity-for-employee-influence_tcm18-33089.pdf

Ferraro, T., Pais, L. & Rebelo dos Santos, N. (2015). Decent work: An aim for all made by all. International Journal of Social Science, IV(3), 30-42.

Foster, B. & Rasmussen, E. (2017). The major parties: National's and Labour's employment relations policies. *New Zealand Journal of Employment Relations, 42(2)*, 95-109

Fryer, G. & Oldfield, Y. (1994). *New Zealand Employment Relations*. Longman Paul.

Greenwood, G. (2016). *Transforming Employment Relationships? Making Sense of Conflict Management in the Workplace* [Unpublished PhD thesis]. AUT University http://hdl.handle.net/10292/9944

Harbridge, R (Ed.). (1993). *Employment Contracts: New Zealand Experiences.* Victoria University Press.

Harris, P. & Twiname, L. (1998). *First Knights: an investigation of the New Zealand Business Roundtable.* Howling At The Moon Publishing.

Kelly, J. (2012). *Rethinking industrial relations: Mobilisation, collectivism and long waves.* Routledge.

Kelsey, J. (1997). *The New Zealand Experiment: A world model for structural adjustment?* Auckland University Press.

Lamare, R., Lamm, F., McDonnell, N. & White, H. (2014). Independent, dependent, and employee: Contractors and New Zealand's Pike River Coal Mine disaster. *Journal of Industrial Relations,* 57(1), 72-93.

McAndrew, I. (2010). The employment institutions. In E. Rasmussen (Ed.). *Employment Relationships: Workers, Unions and Employers in New Zealand* (pp. 74-93). Auckland University Press.

McAndrew, I., Edgar, F., & Jerrard, M. (2018). Human Resource Management and Employment Relations Paradigms in Australia and New Zealand. In J. Parker & M. Baird (Eds.). *Big Issues in Employment* (pp. 1-19). CCH New Zealand.

Rasmussen, E. (2009). *Employment Relations in New Zealand.* Pearson.

Rasmussen, E. (2022). *Employment Relations in New Zealand.* ER Publishing.

Rasmussen, E., & Greenwood, G. (2014). Conflict resolution in New Zealand. In W. K. Roche, P. Teague, & A. J. S. Colvin (Eds.). *The Oxford Handbook of Conflict Management in Organizations* (pp. 449-474). Oxford University Press.

Rasmussen, E. & Lamm, F. (2002). *An Introduction to Employment Relations in New Zealand*. Pearson.

Ravenswood, K. & Kaine, S. (2015). The role of government in influencing labour conditions through the procurement of services: Some political challenges. *Journal of Industrial Relations*, 57(4), 544-562.

Simpkin, G. (2006). Putting Regulation Theory to Work in Industrial Relations. *New Zealand Journal of Employment Relations*, 31(2), 1-16.

Walker, B., & Hamilton, R. T. (2011). Employee–employer grievances: a review. *International Journal of Management Reviews*, 13(1), 40-58.

2. Theoretical frameworks and their application

ERLING RASMUSSEN; FELICITY LAMM; AND JULIENNE MOLINEAUX

1. To define different theoretical standpoints
2. To identify the major frames of reference in employment relations
3. To examine the content of frames of reference and their application
4. To show that the multidisciplinary foundation of employment relations has created theoretical tensions and debates
5. To highlight new theoretical understandings and their employment relations application

Introduction

Employment relations issues are discussed across different academic disciplines and different theoretical approaches have been developed over the years. As in other disciplines, there are different ideas about how certain issues can be explained. Different ideas and opinions are not unique to academia but can be found throughout different parts of society. Most of us have an opinion, one way or the other, about how we work, with whom we want work and how we view those representing our interests and the interests of the other parties. Often our opinion is shaped by where we stand in the organisation's hierarchy. Management and worker ideologies and attitudes are important because they determine the way we behave. For example, a dispute over pay will normally be seen in totally different ways by an employer and by workers. The employer may view a pay rise for workers in terms of less profit for the firm or reducing investment plans while the workers may see the pay rise as necessary for them to pay their bills and as a rightful reward for working hard.

> An ideology is a belief system that describes the way we think about certain things. Our opinions and views on different issues are typically affected by our upbringing, gender, ethnicity, level of education, and so on. Ideology also often refers to certain political belief systems.

These different ways of seeing employment relations are called *frames of reference* or ideologies and are useful tools to help us understand both what is occurring in the employment relationship and also in respect of wider employment relations issues. As there are different and competing frames of reference and ideologies, no single approach satisfies everyone. Some view the workplace as a microcosm of our society with continual tension between employers and employees. Others view organisations as integrated and harmonious collections of people working towards a common goal. Still others see employment relations as a system containing a set of beliefs governed by rules and procedures. These frames of reference have been developed to help us understand events and behaviours that occur in employment relations.

In this chapter, we shall look at the four main theoretical approaches, keeping in mind the strengths and weaknesses of each of them. The chapter begins with a brief presentation of the systems approach. This is followed by an overview of the conflict frames of reference with an emphasis on the traditional three versions: pluralism, unitarism, radical pluralism. The second part of the chapter highlights the multidisciplinary foundation of employment relations and show how new theories and research angles have influenced our current understanding. We show how such theories can be applied to particular problems or issues and exemplify how this can broaden our understanding of employment relations.

Systems approach

One influential work is John Dunlop's 1958 book entitled *Industrial Relations Systems* (see also the updated version, Dunlop, 1993). Dunlop argues that it is useful to treat employment relations as a *system* in order to analyse and interpret the widest possible range of employment practices. Employment relations are seen as a distinctive system although one that partially overlaps and interacts with social, economic and political systems. The focus in the systems approach is to establish and maintain *stability* and *order* in a changing environment and it emphasises the interdependencies and interactions between organisations and their environment. In the context of employment relations, the core feature of this system is, according to Dunlop, a system of rules.

Figure 2.1 shows a system model of employment relations, with inputs that through different processes result in outcomes. The *inputs* include three parts, namely actors, context and ideology. The actors refer to a hierarchy of managers and their representatives as well as a hierarchy of non-managerial employees and their representatives. As these two actors often have competing interests the role of the state, as the third actor, is to balance the power between employers and employees. *Context* refers to the economic, political, and social conditions and how, for example, a political election and the economy impacts upon employment opportunities and working conditions. *Ideology* in this context refers to certain ideas and beliefs regarding the interaction between aforementioned actors.

The *processes* in the systems approach refers to different activities that are often discussed and analysed in the field of employment relations. These processes refer to, for example, bargaining, negotiation, conciliation, arbitration and other examples of state intervention. Finally, inputs and processes result in *outcomes* of the system. The outcomes are, according to Dunlop, two types of rules, namely substantive rules – those that set out the conditions under which people are to be employed, found in for example legislation as well as employment agreements – and procedural rules – that govern how the substantive rules are to be made and interpreted (that includes, for example, processes for negotiation and conflict resolution).

Substantive rules are concerned with what is negotiated and set out the conditions under which people are to be employed.

Examples of substantive rules are agreements about wages, holiday pay, and leave entitlements and can be found in legislation.

Substantive rules can also be the result of bargaining and negotiation between employers and employees and can be found in an individual or collective employment agreement.

Finally, substantive rules can also be less formal rules. For example, work practices and expectations (for example weekly expected outputs from employees) as well as management rules and directives.

Procedural rules are concerned with *how* substantive rules are to be made and interpreted. Examples include how collective bargaining is carried out, as well as how an employee can raise a personal grievance.

Dunlop's systems approach has been extensively critiqued, in particular for placing too much focus on description of what is existing rather than explaining why there are certain tensions between different actors. Conflict is taken as a natural part of employment relations and the systems approach does little to attempt to explain why there is conflict. Another criticism is that it does not adequately discuss the role of power in the employment relationship. This is problematic, as the power struggle between employer and employee interests can be seen as a fundamental part of the employment relationship.

Although Dunlop's system approach has been criticized, it has had an immense influence on the understanding of employment relations. It has, for example, influenced our definition of employment relations (see Chapter one) where concepts such as *rules, processes, contexts and key parties* are used. Further, the systems approach is often used in comparative employment relations, where this framework enables comparison between different national employment relations systems. For example, processes of conflict resolution processes or collective bargaining coverage are issues that can be compared using a systems approach.

Figure 2.1 Dunlop's model of an employment relations system

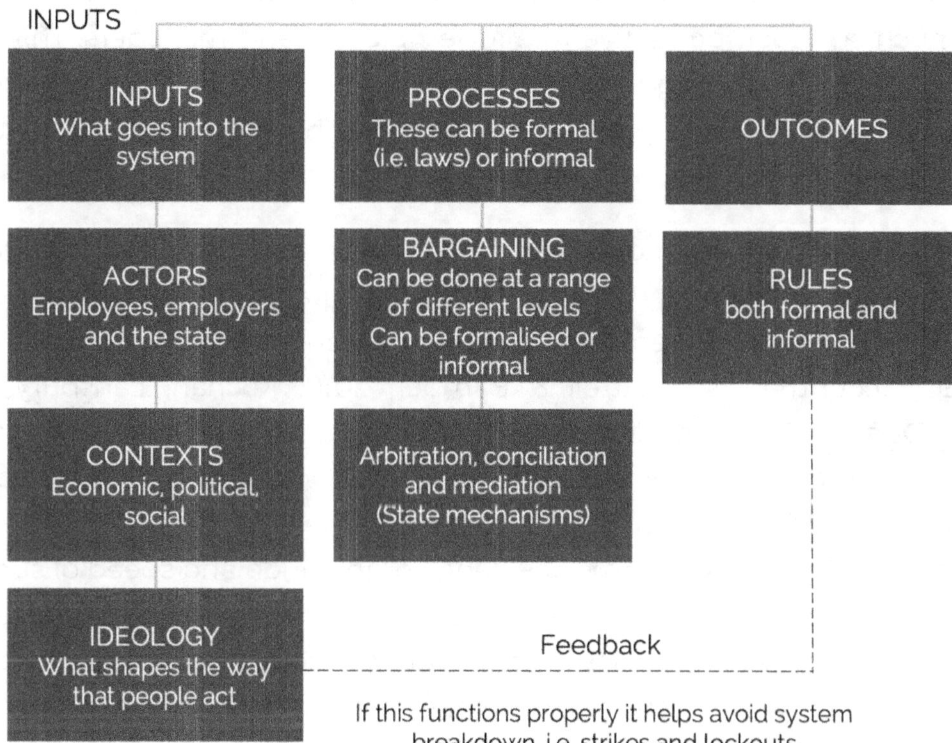

While the thinking and elements of Dunlop's system model can be detected in many discussions of 'national employment relations systems' there have also been distinct attempts to employ insights in other theoretical developments. In light of more pro-active employer strategies and interventions, several American researchers developed new bargaining approaches and understandings of employment relations processes. The Strategic Choice Model, presented in Figure 2.2, is clearly inspired by Dunlop's system model but it is also influenced by the rise of employer power and human resource management practices.

As can be seen from Figure 2.2, the Strategic Choice Model presents a model, just as Dunlop's system model, that can be applied to a national employment relations system. There is also a focus on actors, contexts and bargaining which provide the general settings for employment relations. This allows the model to be applied to different countries. However, there are also major differences as the Strategic Choice Model incorporates a distinct workplace or firm perspective and allows for a much stronger, pro-active role for employers and managers. This is highlighted in the model when it focuses on four different types of employment relations processes that clearly have some affinity with traditional human resource management areas.

The strategic choice model had two further important implications. First, it was associated with a number of comparative industry studies which reviewed key people management trends across a number of OECD countries (see Gittell & Bamber, 2010; Kochan, Lansbury & MacDuffie, 1997; Regini, Kitay & Baethge, 1999). These studies highlighted how, within specific industries, general trends spread across many OECD countries while, at the same time, there are distinct national differences in terms of extent, combination and speed of such industry changes. Second, Katz and Darbishire (2000) have suggested that the patterns of changes were resulting in 'converging divergences' across and within countries. While the spread of technology, managerial strategies and internationalization were amongst some of the influences which led to industry convergence *across* countries – for example, similar approaches in the car manufacturing industry – there were also growing divergences *within* countries. These divergences were driven by different industry employment relations approaches where, for example, the financial sector would have different employment standards and approaches to those existing in the fast-food sector.

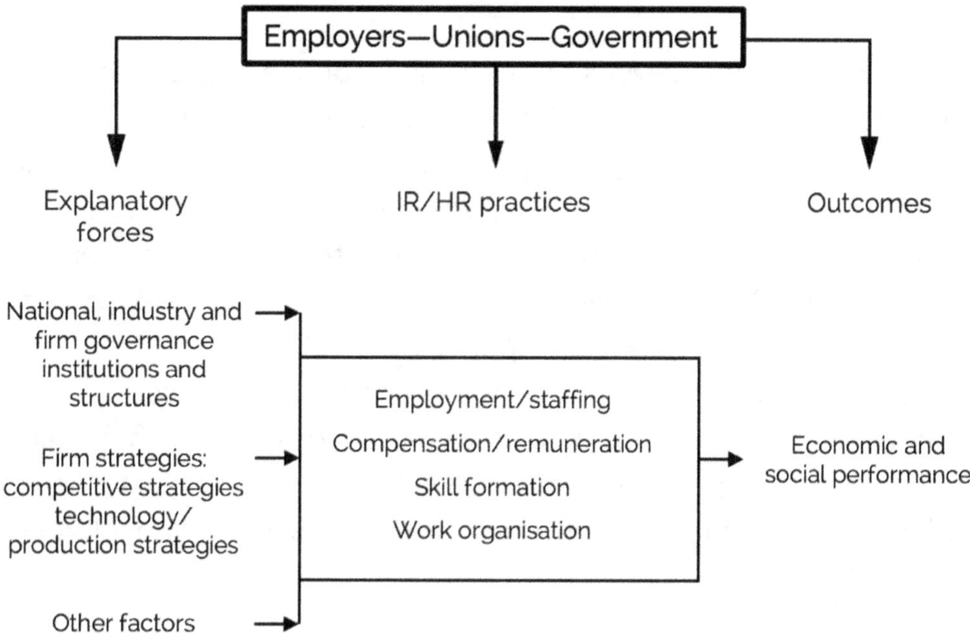

NOTE: Within any single country industrial relations/human resources (IR/HR) practices vary across industries, firms and over time, and all the variables in the model may be shaped by different combinations of employer, union and government influence.

Source: Adapted from an original in Kochan, Locke & Piore (1992)

As discussed above, Dunlop's system model highlights the importance of *rule-making*. Recent studies have been taken this argument further in analysing legislative frameworks and how rule-making "gives priority to the processes of rule-making embodied in and promoted by national labour laws." (Bray & Stewart, 2013, p. 21). This allows an evaluation of the legal hierarchy and regulatory priority of rule-making processes associated with different legislative frameworks, including both the rule-making processes and the application of rule-making evaluations (see Bray & Stewart, 2013; Rasmussen, Bray & Stewart, 2019). In summary, the Dunlop model views employment relations as a distinctive system which is useful in order to analyse and interpret the widest possible range of employment practices.

Conflict frames of reference approach

It is argued that the systems approach is inadequate and that there is a need to dig beneath the surface elements of employment relations, such as collective bargaining, management decision making, legislation, representation and workplace custom and practice. The systems approach has a tendency to ignore the tension that exists in the relationship between the employer and the employee or to treat it as a combination of individual responses and actions. Conflict theorists, on the other hand, are united by their recognition that conflict exists in the workplace. However, their views of the ways in which conflict is manifested, managed and resolved, differ (see Figure 1.3). The following sections outlines three main frames of reference: unitarism, pluralism, radical pluralism.

Unitarism

The unitary frame of reference does not recognise major divergent interests amongst individuals in the workplace. Those who advocate the unitary frame of reference assume that each employee identifies with the aims of the company and with its methods of operation. For this reason, there should be no divisions or conflict of interest between managers and employees because it is in everyone's interest to have efficient production, high profits and good pay.

Unitarism is a perspective that views an organisation as a *team,* in which everyone shares the same goal – which is the success of the organisation. Since the view is that everyone shares the same goals, management has the legitimate role and power to make any decisions. Conflict is seen as sign of communication failure or misunderstandings. Unions are seen as unnecessary.

The unitarist frame of reference has a couple of implications. In the first place, the source of authority lies with management. This view legitimises management prerogative within the workplace and, therefore, management as the sole decision maker. Good employment relations equate with good business and therefore authority can be left in the hands of management. Employees, on the other hand, are motivated by the need to keep their jobs and are not expected to challenge managerial decisions or their employer's right to manage. Employers also believe that it is unacceptable that there should be a third party intervening in the direct employer-employee relationship. Therefore, trade unions are viewed as an unwanted intrusion, creating unnecessary conflict in an otherwise harmonious working environment (see Table 3.2 in Bray et al., 2018, p. 54).

Since the 1980s unitarist ideology has become more refined and is often referred to as 'neo-unitarism' where it has found its way into many New Zealand organisations both publicly and privately owned. Amongst most OECD countries, there has been a trend of weaker unions and less collective bargaining and the resultant employer and managerial confidence in their workplace governance (Foster et al., 2013). Neo-unitarism's main aim is to integrate employees, as individuals, into their organisations where they will become loyal, committed to quality production, customer needs, and job flexibility. Managers, who subscribe to this frame of reference, seek to create a sense of common purpose and corporate culture, set targets for their employees, and invest in training and management development. Techniques to facilitate commitment, quality and flexibility include performance-related pay, profit sharing and employee involvement (Stone et al., 2018). A more sinister version can be found in the so-called 'egoist' version of unitarism, developed by John Budd and his colleagues, where a market-orientated, individualised approach can be aligned with unbalanced employment relationships (see below).

Interestingly, the rise of neo-unitarism in New Zealand has coincided with an increase in the number of human resource managers, many of whom advocate the neo-unitarist view, according to Haworth (1990). It is also suggested that the Employment Contracts Act not only epitomised the neo-unitarist ideology but also accelerated its embeddedness in workplace employment practices (see Chapter 3).

Pluralism

In the 1960s, there was a distinct reaction against the systems approach. Based on research done at Oxford University, employment relations theorists, such as Hugh Clegg, Alan Fox and Allan Flanders, argued that employment relations are much more than a single system held together by one ideology and individuals and groups pursuing their own goals, yet each is dependent upon the others for mutual survival. The collective means by which individuals pursue their goals is not only natural, but also valid. Conflict is accepted as both inevitable and legitimate within any organisation and is tempered and controlled through structures and procedures (see Table 3.3 in Bray et al., 2018, p. 60).

Pluralism is a perspective that views an organization as an entity that holds individuals with different and competing goals which, at the same time, are dependent upon each other for mutual survival. The fundamental unequal power relationship between employers and employees is acknowledged. Trade unions are seen as important representatives of employees and can be of assistance when conflicts in the workplace appears. Although trade unions are given the right to challenge management, the ultimate decision-power rests with management.

The potential conflict that exists between employers and employees can be eased by recognising and involving trade unions. Pluralists argue that greater stability can be achieved by working with trade unions than by outlawing them. Although trade unions are viewed as the legitimate representatives of employees with the right to challenge management, there is still the notion of managerial prerogative. That is, that employers have the legitimate right to manage and to require loyalty from their staff, but must include the other interest groups in the decision-making process.

While pluralists would agree with the radical pluralists and Marxists that society is neither static nor harmonious, they would argue, however, that it is possible to achieve relative stability and accord through negotiation, concession and compromise between the different interest groups. Therefore, organisations have to accommodate different and divergent groups in order to accommodate change. In addition, there is a rough equality of power between the different groups which is adjusted by both formal rules such as legislation and informal work or union rules. Power should be diffused among the main bargaining groups so that no one party dominates the other. Rules and laws should restrain the abuse of power and should enable all parties to accomplish some gains. Also, the role of the government should be to protect the weak and restrain the power of the stronger interest groups.

However, the pluralist approach concentrates on controlling and resolving conflict, rather than on understanding why it is generated in the first place (Bray et al., 2018, p. 61). That is, pluralism offers no comprehensive explanation for industrial conflict, beyond acknowledging that different interests prevail in the workplace. Although pluralism recognises that there is an imbalance of power at the corporate and workplace level, it assumes that there is an approximate balance of power at the national level, with the government acting as neutral referee (see Chapter 10 in Rasmussen, 2009). As a result, pluralists have a tendency to focus on how conflict can be managed while ignoring the nature or basis of conflict.

Radical Pluralism and Marxism

Based on the political economy work of Karl Marx, radical pluralism and Marxism offer a different perspective on our understanding of society and employment relations (Bray et al., 2018: 66-70). Radical pluralists and Marxists treat society as fundamentally polarised into two classes: the employers (or capital) and employees (or labour).

This class polarisation is based on the mutual incompatibility of their interests. Radical pluralists and Marxists maintain that the interests of the employers are not legitimate but exploitative. Since employers own the means of production (that is facilities, technology, tools, and machinery) and have power over employees (also referred to as managerial prerogative), who can only sell their labour (time and effort) for wages, there is an inherent inequity in the distribution of rewards in favour of employers (that is employers and owners of a company receive the surplus). Also, any government in a capitalist society will inevitably protect the interests of the powerful and maintain the structural features of society that are crucial to the employers' existence, for example through tax cuts and incentives to invest. The government will control employment conflict through adjudication, mediation and the courts in order to advance employers' interests while at the same time playing a decisive role in defeating strikes through the use of the law.

Radical Pluralism is a perspective that views industrial conflict as an aspect of class conflict in the wider society. As long as one class owns the means of production (capital, or employers) the other class that is relying on wages for their survival (employees) will be exploited. The state cannot do much as long as the economic system of capitalism remains. In fact, the state is often said to be an important actor of maintaining the status quo and the promotion of the interests of employers.

Radical pluralists and Marxists argue that conflict is inherent in employment relations for two reasons. Firstly, our society is class-based and ownership acts as a source of power and control. This gives employers, who own the means of production, the right to employ workers and direct how they shall work (Frege, Kelly & McGovern, 2011). The resulting conflict between employers and employees has become institutionalised, with bargaining agents and a set of parameters laid down by the state and judiciary. Also, the vulnerability of employees as individuals invariably leads them to form trade unions in order to protect their own interests. Trade unions, while they cannot resolve conflict, are viewed as the inevitable consequence of the employers' exploitation of employees (Bray et al., 2018). Secondly, since the workplace mirrors our society, individuals will have differing values, interests and objectives. Therefore, employers and employees will have different attitudes and beliefs and, in turn, these will create tension and ultimately conflict between the two camps.

However, radical pluralist and Marxist theories are criticised because they are based on ideas developed in the 19th century and as a result are seen to have little relevance for the 21st century. Critics maintain that the growth of middle management and professionals does not exactly fit in with the simplistic view that the working environment is divided into two groups – employers versus employees (for new insights on management theory, see Cummings et al., 2017). It is argued that because radical pluralist and Marxist analysis is predominantly directed at identifying the source of conflict, it has difficulty in recognising other potential outcomes of employment relations. The pluralist and Marxist view is that changes in the structures and institutions will create changes in the relationship between the employer and employee. However, others argue that this will not automatically occur. That is, there has to be a succession of changes in society at large before changes in the fundamental aspects of employment relations are likely to take place.

The application of frames of reference

New Zealand's employment legislation from the early Industrial Conciliation and Arbitration Act 1894 to the Labour Relations Act 1987 aimed to control and institutionalise conflict (see Chapter 3). The dominant employment relations orthodoxy during that period, and particularly in the 1960s and 1970s, was pluralism with its consensus politics, tripartite relations amongst government, employers and trade unions, and collectivism dominating employment relations (Williamson, 2016). At the corporate level, employment relations were controlled by industrial relations managers who often started as union delegates and typically worked their way up within the organisation structure.

Table 2.1 Frames of reference

Theory	Management	Workers	Unions	Conflict	The state
Unitarism	Legitimate source of authority	Resources to be applied to production process	Outside intrusion into relationship between firm and employee	Unnecessary and incompatible with the aims of the organisation	Should provide a minimal framework but has no special interests in the employment relationship
Pluralism	Co-ordinator of a coalition of interests	Partners in production	Legitimate representative of workers' interests	Inevitable – can be resolved positively by an institutional framework that encourages consensus	Acts as the referee by providing institutions to resolve conflict; represents 'the public good'
Radical pluralism	Exploiter	Exploited	Only voice for exploited	Inevitable – will only ever end with the overthrow of capitalism	Coercive arm of capitalism

Source: Rasmussen & Lamm, 2002, p. 17

During the late 1980s and through the 1990s, the pluralist frame of reference shifted more towards a unitarist approach with its emphasis on management prerogative, individualism, freedom of association, workplace bargaining, market-led wage determination and market economy (see Chapter 3). With the passing of 'new-right' employment legislation, such as the ECA 1991, the unitarist frame of reference was further strengthened. It has also been argued that more sophisticated unitarist ideas, promoted by a new breed of Human Resource Managers who are more likely to be university educated, are commonplace in large corporations and the public sector (Haworth, 1990 & 2012).

Different frames of references can also be linked to ideologies and different political parties. For example, employment relations policies by the National Party have often been inspired by unitarist assumptions, which is evident in both the Employment Contracts Act 1991 as well as the post-2008 changes to the Employment Relations Act (see Chapter 4). Traditionally, the Labour party has developed and promoted pluralist policies, of which the ERA 2000 is one example. However, an exception to the rule is how the Labour Government in the 1980s adopted market-based policies, sold state-owned assets and adopted more of a unitarist approach (see Chapter 3).

There have also been several important ways of developing the theoretical basis of frames of reference. Following the lead of Fox (1974), there have been different typologies that aim to explain how different management styles and strategies can impact on employment relations. These typologies are often based on managers' attitudes to collectivism (Purcell, 1997; Sisson, 1989; see examples on the website from Rasmussen, 2009: 299). These attitudes have been researched in New Zealand where Geare et al. (2006 & 2009) found that managers had more pluralist attitudes when it concerned employment relations in general but exposed unitarist attitudes when it involved employment relations at their own workplace. This animosity towards collectivism and legislative restrictions on the managerial prerogative was also found in the research by Foster et al. (2009, 2011 & 2013) on the attitudes of New Zealand employers. It can partly explain the significant employer support of curtailing individual and collective employee rights under the 2008–2017 National-led governments (see Chapter 4).

Another theoretical development has been to expand the various conflict frames of reference. This has included the suggestion of a new neo-liberal, market-orientated management approach, called 'egoist' by Budd and Bhave (2008), illustrated by Table 2.2 below. This maybe a suitable addition in light of the decline of traditional employment relationships in many OECD economies (see Chapter 6). It also aligns with the comparative research of Baccaro and Howell (2011 & 2017) which finds that employer discretion has grown across OECD countries. Although Baccaro and Howell do not rely on frames of reference, their findings could be seen to provide a comparative, empirical support of the growing importance of egoist and neo-unitarist frames of reference since the 1980s.

Table 2.2 Alternative approaches to the employment relationship

Approach	Key points of analysis	Ideological perspective
Neo-classical economics	Rational economic decisions by individuals based on market prices	Egoist
Human resource management	The organizational leadership and policies required to satisfy the psychological needs of employees	Unitarist
Marxism	Class struggle and control within the labour process	Radical
Employment relations	The rules that regulate the employment relationship	Pluralist

Source: Bray et al., 2018, p. 17

In collaboration with other colleagues, John Budd has subsequently developed the conflict frames of reference further (see Budd, Colvin & Pohler, 2020) where interesting new angles are the application of these frames on employer and employee attitudes and linking them to diverse response patterns and conflicting interests. The frames of reference can also be intertwined with the traditional distinction between efficiency and equity (as explained below). For example, Budd and Colvin (2013: 13) have suggested that "the trilogy of efficiency, equity, and voice is a useful framework for considering the goals of conflict management in organization." Overall, these developments of the conflict frames of reference draw on a number of multidisciplinary perspectives and insights and indicate how such multidisciplinary perspectives can be fruitful in adjusting theoretical understandings.

Multidisciplinary perspectives

Understanding different disciplinary perspectives is important in the study of employment relations for a number of reasons. First, it is important when reading employment relations texts or research reports to recognise the assumptions that the authors may be making and the particular biases, conscious or unconscious, that they may bring to the discussion of their subject matter. Secondly, it is necessary to recognise one's own biases in approaching the study of employment relations – biases that may be derived from earlier courses of study in law, or economics, or sociology, or that may stem from particular work experiences, political attitudes and philosophies, or family and group pressures. Let us not imagine that we can eliminate such biases or indeed that we should strive to do so. Thirdly, it is necessary is to articulate our biases, to examine the ways in which they are likely to influence our approach to employment relations, and to understand how they may colour our discussions of employment relations issues. This articulation also allows other people to understand and evaluate our approach to employment relations.

There may be a variety of points of view on any single employment relations issue. As shown in Table 2.1, such points of view are often determined by the particular discipline that the observer or analyst is drawing upon. Let us look, for example, at the ways in which industrial stoppages may be 'explained' by the economist, the psychologist, the sociologist, the political scientist, and the lawyer. Table 2.1 caricatures some of the different perspectives that exist as each specialist seeks to explain a particular phenomenon – in this case the phenomenon of industrial stoppages (that is a strike if initiated by the employees, and a lockout if initiated by employers) – from within the frames of reference provided by his or her discipline. Moreover, within any single discipline there will be widely divergent ideological and philosophical positions as to the 'cause' of work stoppages.

Above all, it is important to understand that the most crucial aspect of the different disciplinary perspectives and personal biases that we each bring to the study of employment relations is that they determine the information we seek out, the methods of investigation we adopt, and the models we have in mind regarding the kinds of change that should be made in the practice of employment relations. For example, the economist in seeking to 'explain' industrial stoppages will look for some relationship between strike statistics and general economic indicators. He or she will want to know whether industrial stoppages increase or decrease significantly with changes in the level of employment, with changes in the rate of inflation, with changes in real disposable incomes or with changes in some other index of economic activity. Should some such significant relationship emerge from such research, the economist is likely to advocate courses of action by government to deal with problems of unemployment, inflation, or personal taxation in the expectation that policy changes in these areas will have some impact on industrial stoppages.

The psychologist, in contrast, in seeking to 'explain' industrial stoppages, will collect totally different kinds of data – his or her research being designed perhaps to establish whether or not there is some relationship between the numbers of industrial stoppages and the extent to which individual employees are satisfied with the nature of their work. The psychologist, too, will prescribe changes based on the evidence collected, except that his or her prescription is likely to be aimed at creating a more positive psychological relationship between the individual and the work that he or she does. The expectation is that the key to reducing the number of industrial stoppages lies in workplace relationships rather than in general economic, social, or political factors.

In essence, illustrating how each specialist discipline tends to define employment relations issues in a *partial* manner; how each collects and analyses information on the basis of restricted initial assumptions, and subsequently proposes policies or seeks solutions that are in turn a function of the assumptions or frames of reference established at the outset. While the reader should be aware that this selectivity is taking place as a result of the perspectives associated with different disciplines, there is no need to be unduly surprised by it. It is a necessary part of any academic or scientific study that some limitation has to be placed on the facts that are observed and on the information that is collected from the infinite mass available.

Table 2.3 Disciplinary perspectives on industrial stoppages in employment relations

ECONOMICS	Industrial stoppages are expressions of economic self-interest as employees strive to protect themselves against inflationary threats to their wages. Which employees will be involved in such stoppages will be determined largely by the bargaining power at their disposal; this bargaining power is, in turn, a result of imperfections in the labour market and the monopoly of skills by groups of employees.
PSYCHOLOGY	Industrial stoppages arise as a result of the behavioural eccentricities of the disputing parties, their inability to handle personality clashes, and their poor interpersonal relationships. The alienation of the employee from his or her work, lack of work satisfaction, lack of work motivation, and poor morale are all underlying causes of industrial unrest, as are outdated and inappropriate styles of management and supervision.
SOCIOLOGY	Industrial stoppages are the inevitable consequence of class and status divisions within our society and of the conflict of values between management's demands for efficiency and the employee's demands for fairness and equality of treatment. The growth of large-scale impersonal enterprises and organisations, and the extensive division of labour in those organisations, has increased the gap between management and workforce and accelerated overt forms of conflict.
POLITICAL SCIENCE	Industrial stoppages are the result of the differential distribution of power within industry and are the means by which the parties seek to impose control over each other. In some cases such stoppages may be part of broader political programmes or may arise because of politically motivated leadership within the trade union movement or within employers' organisations.
LAW	Industrial stoppages are the result of the lack of effective disputes procedures, the inadequacies of the government's mediation and conciliation machinery, and the disrespect of the disputant parties for the legal institutions and procedures available to them to resolve their differences.

Source: Rasmussen, 2009, p. 34

Multidisciplinarity fosters theoretical tensions and dynamic growth

As Table 2.3 indicates there is a range of subject areas generated and influenced by the various disciplines. The legal perspective is clearly dominant in employment law. Because of the importance of the country's long-standing statutory system of conciliation and arbitration, the legal perspective has had a particularly dominant influence on New Zealand's employment relations traditions. Legal ideas and views impact on our current employment relations both through the precedents in common and employment law and through the various legislative frameworks that have been adopted over the years. The impact of economics on employment relations has been equally profound and many of the original pioneers of employment relations were economists. Key debates on the functioning of the labour market, on the economic impacts of unions and employment relations institutions, and on labour market flexibility have been driven and dominated by economists. In other areas, it is political theories and the viewpoints of political scientists and political philosophers that take centre stage; especially those dealing with the role of the state in employment relations.

It is important to stress that the multidisciplinary foundation of employment relations ensures that the topic and its research is forever changing. It is also the reason why, as mentioned in chapter 1, there are many ambiguities and unresolved issues since the various disciplines and the changing ideas within these disciplines constantly brings new angles to bear on the subject. There is an ongoing contest of ideas and explanations and this contest means that there is a useful debate in many areas of employment relations when it comes to explain particular issues and trends. These debates ensure a dynamic growth of the employment relations topic as illustrated in chapters 3 to 6. However, the downside is, as stressed in chapter 1, that employment relations becomes near impossible to cover in its entirety. There are always new issues, new explanations and new theoretical developments.

While the multidisciplinary nature of employment relations brings about a contest of ideas and theoretical angles, these ideas, models and theories do not appear out of thin air; they are normally grounded in fundamental economic, social and employment changes. These changes can be prompted by the business cycle, by fundamental labour market changes, by adjustments in social norms or by new technological breakthroughs. For example, the rise of the debate of work-life balance in the new millennium is based on fundamental economic, social and labour market changes: the influx of women in the labour market has been of key importance as have the changing family patterns; economic growth and rising living standards have been confronted with changing income and material expectations; the promise of new technology and economic growth bringing shorter working time contrasts with some people working very long hours and a considerable diversity in working time patterns. Thus, the very similar notion of work-life balance is rather complex as it can be viewed from many angles and its relevance has been prompted by fundamental societal changes. In the following, we will present an overview of some of these debates and theories that tend to cut across different disciplines.

As mentioned above, the *two key 'labour issues'* at the turn of the twentieth century were social order and social welfare. In New Zealand, these issues were associated with major industrial and political upheaval in the 1890s which prompted the introduction of the world's first national conciliation and arbitration system in New Zealand in 1894 (see Chapter 3). The conciliation and arbitration system was primarily a way of ensuring social order – controlling strikes and lockouts – but its wage-fixing properties also contributed to beneficial working conditions and thus impacted on social welfare. The conciliation and arbitration system was a radical development but it also encapsulated fundamental issues associated with legal employment relations frameworks: what should the role and functions of the state be, how could collective bargaining and unions contribute positively (or viewed negatively: the effects be constrained), what kinds of dispute resolution would be most effective? As conditions and power balances changed, the 'solutions' to these issues shifted and new 'solutions' became the order of the day. This has become evidently so in the last 25 years with the legislative frameworks undergoing radical changes (see Chapters 3 & 4).

Chapters 3 to 6 indicate how *the balance between the fundamental guiding principles of 'efficiency and equity'* has shifted over time but also how the understandings underpinning the delivery of efficiency and equity have adjusted. These understandings have been influenced by the prevailing thinking of the day, but New Zealand employment has witnessed, in at least three instances, the implementation of radical solutions which has created considerable overseas interest. The main periods of 'experimentation' have been the 1890s, 1930s and 1990s. Faced with relative economic decline, New Zealand's legislative framework has focused more on economic efficiency in recent decades. This has been capsulated in the prime objective of the ECA 1991 being an 'efficient labour market' and subsequently the prime objective of the ERA 2000 being 'productive employment relationships'. Recent public policy fluctuations have also been prompted by changing opinions regarding *how* to obtain higher economic efficiency and how to best balance efficiency with fair bargaining and the protection of workers with limited labour market power (see Chapter 4 to 6). These changing opinions are also associated how higher productivity growth can be enhanced by more worker engagement, involvement and 'voice' (Budd & Colvin, 2013; Rasmussen & Tedestedt, 2017).

Since the early 1980s there has been a major shift in favour of *individualism and workplace employment relations*. While the current legislative framework – see the object clause of ERA 2000 (Figure 4.1 in Chapter 4) – has an explicit promotion of collective bargaining and unionism, a number of statutory individual employment entitlements were also introduced or enhanced and direct, individualised employer-employee relationships still played a crucial role. The focus on individualism has been associated with several interesting theoretical changes.

First, it has questioned the traditional understanding of collective action. With a more heterogeneous and transient workforce, it can often be difficult to fashion collective strategies and campaigns that are inclusive enough. This is a problem that several union movements have faced and new theories have tried to encapsulate how unions have attempted to cover several levels of employment relations (from the workplace to international arena – see Chapter 1) as well as develop a wider agenda which takes into account more social and individual concerns.

Second, the focus on individual behaviour and thinking can be found, as mentioned above, in theories on human resource managements, psychological contracts, emotional and aesthetic labour. These theories emphasise how employees 'feel' and 'think' of, or if seen from an employer's view, *should* 'feel' and 'think'. This can also be found in recent debates about work-life balance, careers and generational differences in work expectations.

Third, anti-discrimination and equal employment opportunity theories and models have prompted considerable changes in employment practices. While these debates may involve a group perspective the legislative interventions have often been about individual employment rights and entitlements.

The focus on workplace employment relations has made human resource management more crucial and also adjusted various human resource management approaches. The growing emphasis on organizational efficiency internationally has coincided with productivity being a major issue in New Zealand employment relations (see Chapter 6). The focus on productivity can also be detected in the recent popularity of strategic human resource management models building on resource-based view of the firm theories (Boxall & Purcell, 2011). This is aligned with the growing emphasis on building human capabilities within organisations and across the labour market. Because of its development mainly in the USA and the UK, the strong Anglo-American bias of human resource management has meant that recent emphasis on employee participation has mainly taken the weak informal, communicative forms (for example, 'employee voice'). This is clearly less powerful when compared to formalised employee participation structures (see Chapter 6).

The popularity of the human resource management approach has been seen by many traditional 'industrial relations' academics as a threat. We regard it as just another example of how the employment relations field of study is continuingly evolving and being enlarged through its multidisciplinary approach. As can be seen from our definitional discussion in Chapter 1 and the multi-disciplinary perspective of this chapter, employment relations span a wide area of interest and covers several levels. In that respect, human resource management becomes a subset of employment relations field of study with its specific focus on organisational and management perspectives (Bray et al., 2018). However, human resource management scholars and practitioners are clearly pursuing their independent, field-specific research interests and thereby contribute to the continuous enlargement of the employment relations field of study. This has also encouraged employment relations scholars to move beyond their traditional focus on union and collective bargaining activities, which has also been prompted by the decline in union membership and collective bargaining in many OECD countries (Bray et al., 2018, p. 9).

Conclusion

This chapter has presented students with different theoretical positions and highlighted the positive impact of having competing position. A major part of the chapter has been devoted to the classical employment relations theories – systems approach and frames of reference (radical pluralism, pluralism, and unitarism) – as they present major research angles and basic understandings. While the discussion of these theories provides its own insights it is the continuous use of them which makes them important. There has been an emphasis, therefore, on providing examples on how the various perspectives are currently applied in employment relations debates. In some cases, this application can be obvious – such as the recent development of frames of reference – while in other cases this is less obvious (such as some of the developments of Dunlop's system theory in comparative employment relations analyses).

The importance of the multi-disciplinary perspectives cannot be overstated as these perspectives have grown strongly in recent years. Different disciplinary perspectives often cloud the debate of employment relations issues as they are responsible for preferences of information sources and research approaches and they can lead to vastly different 'solutions'. While this diversity can be frustrating it also promotes a healthy dose of theoretical debate and tensions which has prompted dynamic growth in theoretical perspectives and their application. It has meant that employment relations research has stayed relevant and forever changing. The drawbacks are that it makes it very difficult for researchers to keep up with theoretical advances and it promotes specialisation which erects barriers for multi-disciplinary understandings.

References

Bacarro, L. & Howell, C. (2011). 'A Common Neoliberal Trajectory: The Transformation of Industrial Relations in Advanced Capitalism'. *Politics & Society*, 39(4), 521–564.

Baccaro, L. & Howell, C. (2017). *Trajectories of Neoliberal Transformation: European Industrial Relations since the 1970s*. Cambridge University Press.

Bamber, G.J. & Lansbury, R.D. (Eds.). (1998). *International and Comparative Employment Relations: A Study of Industrialised Market Economies*. Allan & Unwin.

Bray, M., Waring, P., Cooper, R. & Macneil, J. (2018). *Employment Relations*. 4th Edition, McGraw-Hill Education.

Bray, M. & Stewart, A. (2013). What Is Distinctive about the Fair Work Regime? *Australian Journal of Labour Law*, 26(1), 20–49.

Budd, J. & Bhave, D. (2008). Values, ideologies, and frames of reference in Industrial Relations. In Blyton. P., et. al. (Eds.). *The Sage Handbook of Industrial Relations* (pp. 92-113). Sage Publications.

Budd, J.W. & Colvin, A.J.S. (2013). The Goals and Assumptions of Conflict Management. In Roche, W. K., Teague, P. & Colvin, A. (Eds.). *Oxford Handbook of Conflict Management* (pp. 449-474). Oxford University Press.

Budd, J.W., Colvin, A.J.S & Pohler, D. (2020). Advancing Dispute Resolution by Understanding the Sources of Conflict: Towards an Integrated Framework. *Industrial & Labor Relations Review*, 73(2), 254-280.

Burke, R.J. & Richardsen, A.M. (2019). *Creating Psychologically Healthy Workplaces*. Edward Elgar Publishing.

Boxall, P. & Purcell, J. (2011). *Strategy and Human Resource Management*. Palgrave Macmillan.

Cummings, S., Bridgman, T., Hassard, J. & Rowlinson, M. (2017). *A New History of Management*. Cambridge University Press.

Deeks, J., Parker, J. & Ryan, R. (1994). *Labour and Employment Relations in New Zealand*. Prentice Hall.

Dibben, P., Klerck, G., & Wood, G. (2011). *Employment relations: a critical and international approach*. Chartered Institute of Personnel and Development.

Dunlop, J.T., (1958). *Industrial Relations Systems*. Harvard Business School Press Classic.

Dunlop, J.T. (1993). *Industrial Relations Systems: Revised Edition*. Harvard Business School Press.

Foster, B., Murrie, J. & Laird, I. (2009). It Takes Two to Tango: Evidence of a Decline in Institutional Industrial Relations in New Zealand. *Employee Relations*, 31(5), 503-514.

Foster, B., Rasmussen, E., Laird, I. and Murrie, J. (2011). Supportive legislation, unsupportive employers and collective bargaining in New Zealand. *Relations Industrielles/Industrial Relations*, 66(2), 192-212.

Foster, B., Rasmussen, E. & Coetzee, D. (2013). Ideology versus reality: New Zealand employer attitudes to legislative change of employment relations. *New Zealand Journal of Employment Relations*, 37(3), 50-64.

Fox, A. (1974). *Beyond Contract: Work, Power and Trust Relations*. Faber & Faber.

Frege, C., Kelly, J. & McGovern, P. (2011). Richard Hyman: Marxism, trade unionism and comparative employment relations. *British Journal of Industrial Relations*, 49(2), 209-30.

Geare, A., Edgar, F. & McAndrew, I. (2006). Employment relationships: ideology and HRM practice. *International Journal of Human Resource Management*, 17(7), 1190-1208.

Geare, A., Edgar, F. & McAndrew, I. (2009). Workplace Values and Beliefs: An Empirical Study of Ideology, High Commitment Management and Unionisation. *International Journal of Human Resource Management*, 20(5), 1146–1171.

Gittell, J.H. & Bamber, G.J., (2010). High-and low-road strategies for competing on costs and their implications for employment relations: International studies in the airline industry. *International Journal of Human Resource Management*. 21(2), 165–179.

Haworth, N. (1990). HRM – a Unitarist Renaissance? In Boxall, P. (Ed.) *Function in Search of a Future: perspectives on contemporary human resource management in New Zealand* (223-236). Longman Paul.

Haworth, N. (2012). Commentary: Reflections on high performance, partnership and the HR function in New Zealand. *New Zealand Journal of Employment Relations*, 37(3), 65-73.

Katz, H. & Darbishire, O. (2000). *Converging Divergencies*. ILR Press/ Cornell University Press.

Kochan,T.A., Lansbury, R.D. & MacDuffie, J.P. (1997). *After lean production: evolving employment practices in the world auto industry*. ILR Press.

Purcell, J. (1987). Mapping management styles in employee relations. *Journal of Management Studies*, 24(5), 533-548.

Rasmussen, E., Bray, M. & Stewart, A. (2019). What is Distinctive about New Zealand's Employment Relations Act 2000? *Labour & Industry*, 29(1), 52-73.

Rasmussen, E. & Tedestedt, R. (2017). Waves of interest in employment participation in New Zealand. In Anderson, G., with Geare, A., Rasmussen, E and Wilson, M. (Eds.) *Transforming Workplace Relations* (pp. 169-187). Victoria University Press.

Regini, M., Kitay, J. & Baethge, M. (1999). *From Tellers to Sellers*. MIT Press.

Sisson, K. (1989). Personal Management in Perspective. In Sisson, K. (Ed.) *Personnel Management in Britain*. Basil Blackwell.

Stone, R.J. (2018). *Managing Human Resources*. Wiley, 9th Edition.

Williamson, D. (2016). *In Search of Consensus: A History of Employment Relations in the New Zealand Hotel Sector – 1955 to 2000*. PhD Thesis, Auckland University of Technology.

3. Turning points in Employment Relations pre-2000

ERLING RASMUSSEN; FELICITY LAMM; AND JULIENNE MOLINEAUX

1. To present a historical overview of New Zealand's employment relations pre-2000s, and the major changes and conflicts that have taken place over the last century
2. To identify the prevailing economic, social and political ideologies that have shaped employment relations and significant pieces of employment legislation in New Zealand
3. To discuss the impacts of the fundamental shift from a conciliation and arbitration system to decentralised and individualised bargaining processes
4. To identify the changes to employment relations processes and outcomes under the Employment Contracts Act 1991

Introduction

Why are we interested in historical issues and trends when most governments, employers, managers, unions and workers are often focused on current challenges or looking forward to the near future? It is partly that a historical approach can answer the vital question: *how did we end up here?* This is of particular interest in employment relations which is often applied uniquely within national, industry or organisational levels. As such, historical and comparative trends are often used together to establish the relevance of current New Zealand trends and issues. It is also partly about being aware of past mistakes, past public policy directions and biases or negative side-effects of previous employment approaches. Finally, history provides a perspective on current issues whether they are about inequality, unemployment, union density, collective and individual bargaining or any of the myriad of employment relations issues and trends.

The history of employment relations in New Zealand is characterised by change, contest of ideas, political influence and power, and conflict, consensus and conciliation. Its development has been shaped by the prevailing economic, social and political ideologies (Wilson, 2017) and it has been influenced by trends and events in other countries, particularly the UK and Australia. An overview of New Zealand's employment relations history is presented in Figure 3.1, using the major law reforms as historical markers of change. A more detailed overview can be found in Table 3.2 at the back of this chapter. Underscoring employment relations history is the oscillation from a deregulated labour market to a regulated labour market. This movement has not only affected the way New Zealanders have bargained over employment matters, whether on a collective or individual basis, but it has also influenced the balance of power between employers and employees and how workplace employment relations was conducted.

The chapter will describe some of the key turning points of the conciliation and arbitration system and will put emphasis on the 1970s and 1980s where many of the new ideas influencing current employment relations started to surface. As economic and social changes gathered pace in the 1980s, there was considerable pressure on employment relations to adapt to a more open economy, a changing labour force with different aspirations, and turbulent financial markets. While this started to challenge traditional collective bargaining and dispute resolution approaches, the demands for change also covered wider employment relations issues, such as occupational health and safety and equality and discrimination (see Chapter 5).

Finally, we will look in more detail at how employer pressure for further changes, together with a change in political power from a Labour to a National Government, resulted in passing of the Employment Contracts Act 1991 (ECA). The ECA 1991 constituted a 'revolution' of New Zealand employment relations and swept away key features associated with the nearly 100 year-old conciliation and arbitration system. In the era of the ECA 1991, a different employment relations philosophy took hold and, as shown in the next chapter, the ECA has also influenced the current legislation, the Employment Relations Act 2000 (ERA). Thus, we will discuss in more detail the key legislative changes in the 1990s and the major issues, processes and outcomes during this period.

Figure 3.1 New Zealand employment relations timeline

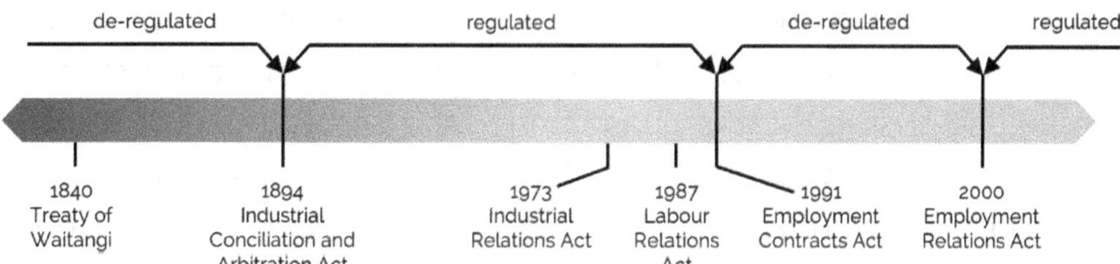

Early conflict

During the 19th century, countries in the northern hemisphere were experiencing enormous upheavals in their political, social and economic structures. In particular, the British economic, political and social systems were not desirable so most immigrants to New Zealand were leaving for a better life. Many of the changes in Britain and Europe were influenced by 'new' technology and the shift from an agrarian-based to an industrial-based economy. These changes created a mass population movement of people to find factory work in towns and cities, but many were deprived of work and this created poverty and crime.

Early colonial settlement in New Zealand was characterised by labour shortages which enabled employees to bargain effectively with their employers for good wages and working conditions. Famously, an employment dispute developed in 1840 over the principle of the eight-hour working day. Samuel Duncan Parnell (1810-1890) is credited for winning this dispute at a time where there were shortages of skilled labour in New Zealand. Parnell was asked to build a store for a local merchant but he refused to work more than eight hours a day. The idea of working an eight-hour day soon spread throughout New Zealand, but it did not become law until 1936.

The period where employees enjoyed good bargaining power was short lived as an economic depression started in the mid-1870s and continued until the late 1890s. The depression period was characterised by high unemployment, deteriorating working conditions and a decline in wages. In response to public pressure over the exploitation of women and children working in factories, the Employment of Females Act 1873 was introduced. The Act focused on working conditions, the hours worked and, most importantly, the health and safety of factories. However, the Act made no provisions for adequate enforcement and, therefore, employers could disregard it, and mistreatment of workers continued at an alarming rate. In 1890, the Sweating Commission was established to investigate the exploitation of New Zealand workers. The Sweating Commission found many examples of poor working conditions and exploitative behaviours. One of the facts that the Commission uncovered was that, when workplaces became unionised, conditions for workers improved, wages did not sink below a living minimum and the hours of work were not excessive.

The Industrial Conciliation and Arbitration system

The new unions were neither experienced nor well-resourced and this made them susceptible to defeat in larger, drawn-out disputes. Their vulnerability was exposed in the trans-Tasman maritime dispute of 1890 which lasted 56 days and involved many industries and workplaces. It originally arose in Australia over the dismissal of a union delegate on a steamship and it quickly spread to New Zealand. The maritime strike was the first major national industrial dispute in New Zealand and ended in complete defeat for unions.

In the aftermath of the maritime strike, there was an overwhelming support from the trade unionists for the Liberal Government in the 1890 election. The new government came into power on a platform of social, political and economic reform. The Liberal Government introduced the structures of a regulated labour market with a legislative programme designed to protect employment conditions and to facilitate wage fixing reforms. The Minister of Labour, William Pember Reeves, introduced the most progressive and comprehensive labour regulation in the world (see below). New Factories Acts were also developed in 1891 and 1894. These Acts required all factories to be registered and it established the Department of Labour and the role of factory inspectors. The Acts gave prominence to occupational health and safety and provided, subsequently, a long-standing legal framework for employment relations, the so-called conciliation and arbitration system.

Industrial Conciliation and Arbitration Act 1894

William Pember Reeves was disenchanted with strike and lockout activity as highlighted by the maritime conflict in 1890 and believed that there had to be a better way of resolving conflict. The Industrial Conciliation and Arbitration (IC&A) Act was designed to facilitate the settlement of industrial disputes by conciliation and arbitration as well as to encourage the formation of industrial unions and employer associations. The major feature of the Act institutes the following bodies and measures:

- **Conciliation Boards.** The country was divided into districts in which Conciliation Boards were elected by employers and employees. Matters could either be referred to these Boards, or a Conciliation Board could conduct its own investigation into disputes. If the decision of the Board proved to be unsatisfactory, or if the Board failed to reach a decision, then either party in the dispute could appeal to the Arbitration court.
- **Arbitration Court.** The court consisted of a Supreme Court judge and two assessors elected by employers' associations and trade unions. The court had power to hand down binding judgment in respect of wage settlement and work conditions. However, the conciliation and arbitration system did not affect farm or non-unionised labour.
- **Registration of trade union.** Unions gained the right to 'exclusive jurisdiction' in an industry if they were registered under the Act. Registration meant that unions became the legally recognised voice of workers. The Act introduced an 'award system', this consisted of the legal employment documents containing details of wage rates and working conditions. Unions were able to take their employers to the Conciliation Boards and the Arbitration Court to obtain awards. However, the unions could not go on strike and thereby put pressure on employers when they were registered under the Act.

The IC&A Act 1894 was intended to stimulate and protect unionism and safeguard the interests of employees. The registration of unions led to great increase in their numbers. The IC&A Act 1894 moved New Zealand from a country with a largely informal employment relations environment to one in which the state offered trade unions powerful statutory means to securing wage settlements with employers. As discussed in the *turning points* below, there were many changes to the original IC&A Act (also beyond those mentioned). It is simplification, therefore, when the IC&A system is presented as a uniform system, running from 1894 to 1991.

Turning point 1: The initial years of the conciliation and arbitration system

Between 1894 and 1906, there were no significant strikes. In the early years of the Arbitration Court, it granted wage increases and improved working conditions. It also facilitated a re-building of the unions and their membership. However, after the turn of the century, the Arbitration Court took an increasingly legalistic and restrictive stand. Some of the complaints from the unions regarding the decisions of the Court were: unfavourable awards, which were cautious, rather than generous, delays in court hearings and failure to conduct factory inspections to see that awards were properly enforced (Holt, 1986). Due to these issues with the IC&A system, there was a growing frustration among workers and trade unionists, and unions started to ignore the non-strike clause in IC&A Act 1894 or deregistered to rely on direct collective bargaining.

This made the conciliation and arbitration system more unstable as unions gained pay rises and better conditions in direct collective action, for example in the 1908 Blackball miners' strike (Binney et al., 1990). Likewise, the First World War (1914-1918) had a major constraining labour market impact, as had various economic downturns and supply issues.

Turning point 2: The 1930s economic depression and reforms by the Labour Government from 1935 onwards

There had been economic stagnation in several years during the 1920s but the fall-out from the Wall Street share market crash turned into a full-blown economic depression during the 1930s. Like most western countries. New Zealand experienced economic decline, very high levels of unemployment, employer pressure to reduce wage levels and widespread poverty. In 1932, the Arbitration Court decided to implement a 10% general reduction in award wages, in line with a similar reduction in public sector wages. A subsequent amendment to the IC&A system also abolished compulsory arbitration which allowed employers to drive through further reductions in wage and working conditions (see Holt, 1986, pp. 185-189).

The Labour Party came to power in November 1935, 19 years after its formation. The newly elected Labour Government soon put through a series of employment reforms. These included restoring the compulsory powers of the Arbitration Court, making union membership compulsory, and allowing the registration of national unions as previously registration had been by district only. Restoring compulsory powers of the Arbitration Court, in effect, restored the Court's authority. This authority allowed Arbitration Court to make legal decisions that often had more to do with the social and economic matters than with the existing employment situation (Deeks et al., 1994, p. 5).

The Arbitration Court decisions between the late 1930s and the mid-1970s were tied to the state benefit and full-time employment policies. This was clearly illustrated by the policy of keeping men in full-time employment at the expense of women's employment (Du Plessis, 1993). In 1937, the Arbitration Court set minimum wages for women, for the first time, at 47% of men's wages. This decision was in keeping with government policy which still maintained that a man, as head of the household, should be primary earner in order to support himself and his family. By 1949, the economy began to stall; the Labour Government ran out of steam after 14 years of being in power and was defeated in the 1949 general election by the National Party.

Turning point 3: The waterside dispute of 1951 and the strengthening of the Industrial Conciliation & Arbitration system

The Watersider dispute of 1951 was larger than all others in New Zealand's employment history (Deeks et al., 1994, p. 52). This dispute was the longest, costliest and most widespread industrial confrontation in New Zealand history and lasted 151 days. When employers refused to pass the full 15% wage increase granted by the Arbitration Court to the waterside workers, the union leaders retaliated and imposed an overtime ban. The port employers threatened to dismiss the workers, who, in turn, responded by walking out.

Prior to the strike, more militant unions (led by the Waterside Workers Union) were angered by the lack of progress on the part of the Arbitration Court to increase wages and improve conditions, and the unions felt resentful about the impotence of the Federation of Labour (formed in 1937). The Federation of Labour backed the Labour Government's economic policy of 'stabilisation' in which the IC&A Act played a key role by delivering static wages and conditions. The Federation of Labour even went so far as to support the National Government to force an end to the strike. However, this unusual position had more to do with supporting the IC&A system and an internal power struggle within the trade union movement than it was an endorsement of the employers' and government's stance. The newly elected National Government declared a state of emergency under the Public Safety Conservation Act and 'brought in servicemen to work the wharves and helped new waterfront unions form under the protection of the police and armed forces' (Deeks et al., 1994, p. 54) and deregistered the striking union.

Overall, many trade unions were dissatisfied with a system that did not allow them to take direct action in the form of strikes. The Arbitration Court worked well for unions in times of economic stability but not in an inflationary economic climate. In addition, the aftermath of the strike saw the penal sections of the IC&A Act strengthened. Strike action became illegal and hazardous for trade unions in terms of financial penalties.

Turning point 4: The Industrial Relations Act 1973

The IC&A system started to experience problems in the 1960s when inflation and full employment encouraged frequent negotiations and more workplace bargaining. The unions were also annoyed that the National Government had introduced voluntary unionism in 1961 (it had been compulsory since 1936). Several unions started to pursue more direct workplace bargaining and, in some cases, they also deregistered from IC&A system and relied on their own bargaining efforts. As a result, so-called 'second-tier agreements' became more significant, especially for larger employers, and this facilitated over-award, decentralised pay rises. The encouragement to pursue workplace bargaining was further enhanced when the Arbitration Court handed down a 'nil order' wage decision in 1968. While the unions and the employer associations managed, in unison, to overturn this decision in favour of a 5% wage decision, it clearly signalled to unions that they could not rely too much on wage increases obtained through the IC&A system.

The Industrial Relations Act 1973 tried to regain control over 'second-tier agreements' by incorporating direct wage bargaining into the legislative structure. Only registered unions could elect to bargain directly with the employer and achieve, subsequently, that these agreements were enforceable by the court. The Act also set fundamental definitional categories for industrial disputes to try to reduce collective action over interpretations of awards and collective agreements:

1. *Disputes of interests* would arise when negotiating an award or a collective agreement. These disputes started a movement towards legalising strikes and lockouts which was further enhanced under

the Labour Relations Act 1987 (see below).

2. *Disputes of rights* occurred when an award or a collective agreement was already in place and the disputes concerned an interpretation of the content of an award or a collective agreement. These disputes were not allowed to be solved through industrial action but had to be dealt with within the Employment Institutions.

However, the Act failed to come to grips with the inflationary pressures fuelled by the 'oil shocks' of the 1970s. Not only did a tight labour market lead to endless bargaining, but the IC&A system became driven more and more by wage relativity considerations (James, 1986). Thus, the National Government became more and more involved directly in collective negotiations in an attempt to keep wage inflation under control.

Turning point 5: Decentralisation under the Fourth Labour Government, 1984-1990

In the early 1980s, economic pressures, many stemming from overseas, impacted strongly on New Zealand's economy. Pressure to change New Zealand's employment relations came from a number of quarters. The Treasury and the Reserve Bank wished New Zealand to progress with changes to bargaining structures and this was also supported by the Business Roundtable and the Employers Federation. The tripartite Long-Term Wage Reform Committee also advocated a more decentralised wage-setting system (Walsh, 1989).

While Australia had instituted an accord between the Labour Government and unions in 1983, public policy took a different direction in New Zealand. Following a sharp devaluation of the New Zealand dollar in the first days of the new Labour Government in 1984, it embarked on a very radical reform programme. These reforms, often called 'Rogernomics' after the Minister of Finance, Roger Douglas, or the 'New Zealand Experiment' (Kelsey, 1997), created a more open economy with reduced state subsidies and taxation and with fewer constraints on activities in most industries. The wave of economic reforms also enhanced pressures to reform employment relations. While the Industrial Relations Amendment Act 1984 had already replaced compulsory arbitration with voluntary arbitration (and thereby taken away the ability of weak unions to force employers to conclude awards and collective agreements), there were demands for further changes to bargaining processes and outcomes. In particular, there were employer demands for decentralised bargaining at enterprise level, changing or abolishing the awards system, and curtailing 'blanket coverage' which extended award coverage to all employers and employees in a particular industry or occupation (Rasmussen et al., 2019).

The Labour Relations Act 1987

The employment relations policy of the fourth Labour Government was based on an uneasy balance between allowing more direct bargaining and retaining the protective mechanisms of the IC&A system. This 'two-handed' approach continued through the 1980s. As a consequence, when the Labour Government introduced its Labour Relations Act 1987 (LRA), some key features of the existing law were retained.

On one hand, the LRA continued with the support of more decentralised bargaining and also supported direct bargaining by making the parties enforce their own agreements, widening the bargaining agenda to allow a greater choice of collective contracts and legalising lockouts and strikes. Employers and unions could also agree to remove themselves from award coverage and instead enter into negotiations of an enterprise agreement. On the other hand, there were considerable regulation of union and bargaining activities and unions were required to have more than a thousand members. Separate Employment Institutions were maintained in the form of a Mediation Service, Arbitration Commission and Labour Court. The

Labour Government also strengthened the statutory minimum wage and introduced, subsequently, legislation on parental leave and pay equity.

In brief, the LRA 1987 could be seen as the gap between the old IC&A system and the employment regime of the 1990s. The LRA 1987 aligned with the Labour Government's wider policy agenda since it shifted employment relations out of government control and into the hands of employers and employees. However, the relatively short existence of the LRA and some union unwillingness to engage in enterprise bargaining meant that the Act did not have much impact in terms of changing bargaining structure, processes and outcomes. Instead, this happened in dramatic fashion under the ECA 1991 (see below).

The state unions and the public sector reforms of the 1980s

Most of this chapter has been devoted to the developments in the private sector. However, it is also important to recognise the ongoing employment relations changes in the public sector. By 1980, more than a fifth of the labour force worked for the government, and the state unions were among the largest and most active in New Zealand. There were several major state unions, with the Public Service Association (PSA), the New Zealand Educational Institute and the Post Primary Teachers Association being the largest. The three distinctive features of public sector unions were the following:

1. Membership was voluntary.
2. Public sector unions operated outside the conciliation and arbitration system and negotiated directly with their employer, the government, and its department heads.
3. Public servants were covered by specific employment legislation, commencing with the Public Service Act 1912 and culminating in the State Sector Act 1988.

Being a government employee or a 'state servant' was considered desirable as there were many benefits for the employees. Some of the benefits included reduced working hours, paid holidays, sickness leave and many others, though these benefits started to be eroded from the 1970s onwards.

The state service unions had been at the forefront of social reform. The PSA had a long history of challenging wage discrimination based on assumptions about women's economic dependency. It also mounted a successful campaign for equal pay in the public service from the mid-1950s, which resulted in the passing of the Government Services Equal Pay Act 1960. This was eventually followed by the Equal Pay Act in 1972, which covered both the public and private sector workers. The continued existence of a gendered labour market made equal employment opportunities important. More than half of all employed women in the 1980s worked in just six occupations groups: nursing, teaching, typing, bookkeeping, cashiers, clerical and sales staff (New Zealand Department of Statistics, 1990). While public servants were pushing for equity between the sexes and ethnic groups and for reforms leading to equal opportunity, in general, they were falling behind in wages compared with their counterparts in the private sector, particularly in terms of managerial wage levels.

As the major economic and social changes were implemented under the Labour Government, this also influenced the public sector with key legislative changes being the State-Owned Enterprise (SOE) Act 1986, the State Sector Act 1988 and the local government reforms of 1989. These Acts aligned employment relations in the public sector with private sector employment relations, including collective bargaining disputes resolution, and the public sector was leading the drift towards bargaining at enterprise level.

The SOE Act 1986 created nine corporate enterprises involved in broadcasting, electricity, forestry, banking, post and telecommunication. This marked the beginning of the dismantling of this part of the public sector, with a loss of more than 40,000 permanent jobs between 1987 and 1989. These changes had profound implications for employment relations and, according to Walsh and Wetzel (1993), it changed the structure of collective bargaining processes and the unions' role in decision making in SOEs. Subsequently, many of the SOEs were privatised (see Spicer et al., 1996).

The State Sector Act 1988 also facilitated a shift from sector to enterprise bargaining. However, the strong coordination role of the State Service Commission meant that the bargaining processes and outcomes changed less, compared to changes amongst the SOEs. Still, the enterprise focus allowed for diverse pay and conditions amongst managerial staff and undermined the notion of a state sector career.

Finally, the 1989 local government reforms amalgamated local government bodies into larger units and also allowed local government bodies more leeway in developing their own economic strategies (see Bush, 1995). This prompted considerable employment relations changes, with more diverse bargaining processes and outcomes, partly resulting from experiments with new employment arrangements and outsourcing of work.

Employment relations in the 1990s

The Labour Government attempted to follow a 'two-handed approach' in the 1980s in order to achieve both a decentralisation of bargaining arrangements and a protection of weak employee groups. Employer pressure for further change, together with a change in political power from a Labour to a National Government, resulted in the passing of the ECA 1991. This represented a dramatic shift in employment relations philosophy, bringing to employment relations the same deregulation and market focus that other parts of the economy had experienced since 1984.

Some of the changes following the ECA's implementation were expected while others were not. The decline in union density and in collective employment contracts followed the predicted path. It was also anticipated that employees in the secondary labour market would fare less well in a deregulated labour market and that there would be a diversity in bargaining outcomes.[1] However, it is difficult to ascertain which changes in bargaining outcomes can be attributed to the ECA 1991, which ones can be attributed to delayed effects of the previous legislative changes, and which could be regarded, as a result of wider economic conditions. Growth in productivity was disappointingly low under the ECA, a surprise to those who blamed New Zealand's low productivity growth on the labour market inflexibilities and union monopolies of the previous regime.

The ECA 1991 made employment law a key employment relations topic in the 1990s. The Act brought the notion of employment *contracts* to the forefront of the debate. As *all* employees had access to minimum employment rights, including the personal grievance option, the distinction between an employee and a contractor became crucial (see Chapter 1). Although the ECA 1991 set the broad parameters for employment relations behaviour in the 1990s, the *non-prescriptive nature* of the Act made case law and the legal precedent-setting important. However, the resulting drawn-out and often confusing changes associated with legal precedent made planning difficult for employers and employees alike. The many cases before the Employment Tribunal indicated a shift towards individualised bargaining and dispute processes and this, in turn, raised the questions of whether such a trend towards litigation was beneficial and whether it would bring about efficient workplace practices. By 1999, the Employment Tribunal had a large backlog of cases, and rulings took up to a year to be delivered (Te Ara, 2018, p. 10).

---

1. The distinction between the 'primary and the secondary labour market' is based on the Dual Labour Market Theory where the 'secondary labour market' is characterised by low status, low pay and often unsure employment, while the 'primary labour market' is associated with high status, high pay, and opportunities for upskilling, career development and promotion (see Rasmussen, 2009, pp. 429-431).

The shift in employment relations philosophy

With the post-1984 economic and social reforms, considerable philosophical debate started about which principles should underpin employment relations. The principles governing employment relations prior to 1984 were derived, in broad terms, from the intellectual tradition associated with Keynesian economic policies, state intervention and welfare state provisions. A tripartite pluralism was often the explicit goal. That is, the state provided a legislative framework which promoted a balance of interests between employers and employees. This was encapsulated in the award structure and its collective bargaining process. It was understood by proponents of that framework that the only context in which individuals could confront, on an equal footing, the relatively more powerful employers in negotiations was through the effective collective organisation of individual employees.

As we saw earlier in this chapter, there was mounting frustration over the inability of the IC&A system to deliver efficient results across the labour market. It became evident in the 1980s that the traditional consensus surrounding employment relations had begun to evaporate and that the latent conflict between centralisation and decentralisation was coming to the fore. A comparison of the basic assumptions of the arbitration system with those of the deregulated labour market approach illustrate interesting philosophical differences. The arbitration system assumed that the employment relationship was a special one – that it differed from a standard market exchange relationship – and that it was one which required some measure of state regulation and involvement (Deeks et al., 1994, p. 82; Walsh, 1993, p. 176).

However, the proponents of labour market deregulation (e.g. Brook, 1990 & 1991) argued that:

- the employment relationship is a private contractual relationship between two parties;

- with the notion of individual choice being promoted, contractual arrangements should have few limits as long as both parties agree;
- beyond supporting fair market exchanges, the state should refrain from labour market interventions;
- supporting fair market exchanges implies restricting or abolishing the monopoly rights of unions.

The question of power imbalance was either not discussed or seen to be solved through other contracting possibilities (for example, having a 'bargaining agent').

Thus, the deregulation approach entailed abandoning the traditional balance between efficiency and equity since market solutions were expected to provide adequate equity outcomes over time. In the rare instances where this did not occur, shortcomings could be better compensated through tax or income transfer policies than through direct labour market interventions. The enactment of the ECA 1991 epitomised this philosophical shift by introducing substantial deregulation of bargaining structures and processes. It rejected many of the principles associated with the IC&A system.

Deregulation of employment relations was relentlessly promoted by the business lobby group, the Business Roundtable (Harris & Twiname, 1998), and found at least some support within many business groups. The favoured outcomes of the Business Roundtable were an 'employment at will' situation with limited or no restrictions on a direct exchange between employer and employee (Walsh & Ryan, 1993).

The Employment Contracts Act 1991

The ECA focused on efficiency and emphasised that parties have wide-ranging choices in terms of organisational affiliation and bargaining arrangements. This was clearly stipulated in the Act's long title:

'An Act to promote an efficient labour market and, in particular

(a) To provide for freedom of association;

(b) To allow employees to determine who should represent their interests in relation to employment issues;

(c) To enable each employee to choose either

> (i) To negotiate an individual employment contract with his or her employer; or

> (ii) To be bound by a collective employment contract to which his or her employer is a party;

(d) To enable each employer to choose

> (i) To negotiate an individual employment contract with any employee;

> (ii) To negotiate or to elect to be bound by a collective employment contract that binds two or more employees;

(e) To establish that the question of whether employment contracts are individual or collective or both is itself a matter for negotiation by the parties themselves.'

The ECA constituted a dramatic shift in employment relations – away from the collectivist traditions of the past – by promoting the rights of individual employees and employers. It abolished the award system and union preference rights, and promoted an enterprise-bargaining model in both private and public sectors. The emphasis on individualism and individual choice was promoted in several ways. It was made explicit in Part I of the Act that the individual had an unfettered choice of whether or not to join a union and no undue influence or preferential treatment were allowed by either employers, employees or unions in order to promote or prevent union membership. The individual focus was also bolstered through the notions of employee representatives ('bargaining agents'), authorisation and ratification of contracts, and personal grievances which all made the individual employee the 'actor'.

The individual focus was further enhanced by making collective bargaining more difficult under the Act. There were a number of new terms concerning authorisation, access to employees, ratification procedures and the extension of collective employment contracts. These new terms made it easy for employers to obstruct the unions' collective bargaining attempts as the unions would have had to clarify the meanings of the new terms through court action. However, the major stumbling block for collective bargaining was that it was unlawful to stage collective action when pursuing a multi-employer contract. This made it near impossible for the unions to continue with industry- or occupation-based multi-employer collective contracts. This restriction was probably in breach of New Zealand's obligations under the International Labour Code (Haworth & Hughes, 1995; Wilson, 2000). It is no wonder, then, that collective bargaining and union density dropped dramatically under the ECA, as detailed below.

However, Walsh (1993) noted that while the ECA greatly diminished the role of statutory regulation of collective bargaining, it did retain and expand a limited range of employment conditions. The Act also covered *all* employees, whether they were on collective or individual employment contracts, and across both public and the private sectors. Previously, employees on individual employment contracts were outside the employment relations framework and, as mentioned above, many 'primary labour market' employees came under labour law jurisdiction for the first time with the passing of the ECA.

The ECA's Employment Institutions were relatively similar to the traditional labour institutions under the IC&A system. It provided a strong role for the existing legacy of legal precedence; procedural fairness was crucial in the area of dismissals; the fines and jurisdiction available were substantial; and personal grievances could relatively easily be pursued through the Employment Institutions (Walsh, 1993; Grills, 1994). It also gave mediation a larger role in dispute resolution.

The growth in personal grievance cases and mediation's larger role meant that the Employment Institutions played a crucial, more politicised role under the ECA (Rasmussen & Greenwood, 2014; Walsh, 1993).

Outcomes: union density and collective bargaining

New Zealand has no regular, comprehensive workplace surveys, making longitudinal assessments of changes in workplace practices and employment conditions harder to establish. In particular, information about trends in the secondary labour market has been limited (McLaughlin, 2000). Thus, one has to be cautious in aligning labour market changes, beyond changes to collective bargaining and union density, to the impact of the ECA.

The ECA led to a decline in union density (union members as a percentage of the workforce). Union membership fell sharply following the ECA's introduction and continued to fall throughout the decade. This decline meant that there was often no union presence in many workplaces in the private sector. In these workplaces, there was no real collective bargaining option available to employees since the expected influx of non-union bargaining agents did not occur. It was only in their traditional strongholds (including the public sector) that the unions kept collective bargaining alive and only there that the unions managed to maintain their representative status.

The advent of the ECA saw changes to bargaining processes and practices, with a move away from collective employment contracts towards individual employment contracts. Prior to the passing of the Act, it was estimated that collective employment contracts covered around 56% to 60% of employees. By February 1992, 45.6% of all those employed were on individual employment contracts, which increased to 56.6% in February 1993 (Statistics New Zealand, 1994, p. 133). Even so, the collective bargaining coverage was probably inflated since it included so-called 'collective contracting' under the ECA; that is, collective employment contracts developed (without union negotiations) by the employer and then signed subsequently by employees (Dannin, 1997; Gilson & Wagar, 1998).

Table 3.1 Unions, membership and density 1985–1999

Month	Year	Unions	Membership	Density
December	1985	259	683 006	43.5%
September	1989	112	648 825	44.7%
May	1991	80	603 118	41.5%
December	1991	66	514 325	35.4%
December	1992	58	428 160	28.8%
December	1993	67	409 112	26.8%
December	1994	82	375 906	23.4%
December	1995	82	362 200	21.7%
December	1996	83	338 967	19.9%
December	1997	80	327 800	18.8%
December	1998	83	306 687	17.7%
December	1999	82	302 405	17.0%

Source: Crawford et al., 2000, p. 294

The level of industrial stoppages was moderate under the ECA, when compared with the situation in the previous decade. The low level of industrial stoppages was probably influenced by the weaker position of the union movement and the fact that the ECA introduced further restrictions on strike actions, including strike action being unlawful in pursuit of a multi-employer collective employment contract. On the other hand, some employers became more aggressive in their negotiation tactics and lockouts, or the threat of lockouts became more important in the first years of the ECA. This included so-called partial lockouts where employees are not locked out of the workplace but the employer withholds one or more of their employment conditions, such as overtime payments, until a settlement is reached. Partial lockouts were first deemed lawful in 1992, but a June 1994 Employment Court decision reversed that legality and, subsequently, occurrence of partial lockouts declined significantly.

Outcomes: the changing status of employment law in the 1990s

The non-prescriptive nature of the ECA meant that there were few directions on how to conduct an employment relationship. As the Act represented a sharp break with the previous conciliation and arbitration system, it contained many new terms which had either vague or no prescribed legal meaning. Therefore, legal decisions taken in the Employment Tribunal, Employment Court and Court of Appeal had a significant impact on the development of employment relations under the ECA.

Reaching legal decisions entails a detailed examination of particular practices and such decisions can establish a well-founded view on a workplace problem over time. However, the constant process of litigation was rather costly (commentators have pointed to lawyers as the major beneficiaries of the ECA – see MacDonald, 1994), and it took considerable time to develop a sufficiently large body of case law to establish benchmarks for the major types of employment relations practices. This also means that individual cases can cause confusion about what is an appropriate, lawful employment relations practice. Under the ECA, this confusion was understandable, since the courts sometimes came to rather different conclusions about similar practices. This was the case in areas of redundancy, fixed-term employment contracts and holidays entitlements and, as highlighted above, it had a significant impact on the use of lockouts in the 1990s.

While the ECA saw a sharp decline in collective bargaining and union density, employees in the 'primary labour market' had more leverage, leading to a high level of individual disputes with personal grievance rights becoming central in employment relations. The Act afforded employees the opportunity to decide themselves whether they would lodge a personal grievance claim, whereas previously, the claims procedure had to be conducted through unions. Well-publicised decisions awarding significant compensation to senior or managerial employees influenced some managers to become more careful regarding substantive and procedural fairness in dealings with their staff.

Under the ECA, the idea of a fair process, also known as *procedural fairness*, received a lot of attention. Key elements of a fair process are a *discussion* of the issues at stake between employer and employee and *issue clarity*. These key elements are important as each party should understand the other's position and also what changes and outcomes are sought. Procedural fairness includes giving the employee the opportunity to rectify the problem and making sure the employee understands that he/she could be dismissed if the problem is not solved. In other words, the employee should be aware of the exact problem and know how to rectify it and be given adequate time to do so (see Chapter 1). In such situations, procedural fairness is important and, if not followed carefully, can lead to a personal grievance being lodged.

The rising number of personal grievance cases in the 1990s and the confusion surrounding justifiable dismissals raised doubts about the efficiency of the non-prescriptive nature of the ECA. This meant that there was a lack of adequate guidelines for satisfactory employer and employee behaviour. Instead, the process of developing legal precedent – that is, court decisions on key legal issues – was used to formulate more precise guidelines. This was a long-winded and litigious process and could be difficult to understand for the average employer and employee.

Outcomes: key labour market changes during the 1990s

When it comes to the changes that occurred in *wages, wage dispersion and other employment conditions* in the 1990s, it is important to stress that these changes were not attributable, either directly or indirectly, to any single factor. The ECA 1991 had an important impact, but so did other changes in the New Zealand economy, such as economic activity and demographic changes. Any suggested causality between trends in labour market indicators and the impact of the ECA needs to be critically examined.

Although average hourly wages increased every year in the 1990s, these increases were initially matched by increases in the Consumer Prices Index for the first part of the 1990s, and then real wages increased slowly in the second half of the 1990s. During the ECA's first two years, the expectation of increased wage dispersion (that is, a growing difference between high and low wage levels) resurfaced in frequent media reports, as did reports of widespread abolitions and reductions in penal rates and overtime payments. The biggest effects of these cuts were felt in those areas of the labour market in which penal rates and overtime payments constituted a major part of wage packages, such as low-wage areas of retailing, hospitality, cleaning and caregiving.

There were major changes in *working hours* in the 1990s, with a tendency towards longer working hours amongst full-time employees and a rise in the number of people working part-time. In the 1990s, the 40-hour working week was no longer the prevailing norm. The workforce was split roughly into three parts, with around a third normally working less than 40 hours, another third working 40 hours and the remaining third working in excess of 40 hours per week. Several indicators pointed to a substantial increase in working time: full-time employees worked, on average, more hours per week; there were more people working very long hours, and there were more people with more than one job. It is difficult to see how this move towards longer working hours can accommodate the fashionable notion of balancing work and family life or allow time for continuous upskilling and re-education.

On the other hand, the number of people working part-time also increased, with female employees accounting for more than two-thirds of this increase. While part-time employment suits many people with family responsibilities, there are negative aspects to it, such as limited income, fewer career prospects and reduced training opportunities. Many employees also found it difficult to plan working hours as casualisation, on-call arrangements and split-shifts became more common (Brosnan & Walsh, 1998). McLaughlin (2000) found in his survey of employees in the retail sector that such employees had a limited choice regarding the scheduling of their working hours and many reported that their hours of work had a detrimental impact on their family life.

While most new jobs created were still full-time ones, there was a strong rise in 'non-standard' types of employment, such as an increase in multiple job holders and people working on either a casual or a fixed-term basis. The number of people employed in both the primary and secondary sectors of the economy declined significantly while employment in the service sector increased by nearly 20%. It was within the expanding service sector of the economy that most non-standard work was created.

An increase in non-standard employment has far-reaching implications for the individuals concerned (Brosnan & Walsh, 1998). It can provide an opportunity to tailor one's working patterns to family or personal interests, it may open the way for new career options and it can be an option when faced with unemployment (Alach & Inkson, 2004). However, it has been suggested that many of the new 'non-standard' work practices may simply be a way for employers to cut costs, with some of these costs and insecurities being passed onto individuals. This has been especially true in the case of self-employed contractors. They are not protected by employment law as they are not classified as employees and, consequently, they are not entitled to related benefits. The costs for the individuals concerned are many and varied and include: unpredictability of income; no payment of mandatory employee-related benefits (e.g. holiday pay, sick pay, statutory holiday pay); no provision of training; limited ongoing professional advancement and development (Burgess & Connell, 2004). In some cases, there are also negative social implications, such as inconvenient or long working hours and the inability to plan family and leisure time.

Unemployment levels fluctuated a great deal under the ECA but stayed at a concerning high level for most of the 1990s. At the same time, there was a sharp increase in the number of people on other types of benefits. Despite changes in employment relations and the benefit cuts of the early 1990s (Boston & Dalziel, 1992), it was necessary for the government to devote further attention to unemployment and social welfare problems. This included the 1995 Employment Task Force reports, the 1998 'work fare' scheme for unemployed people, and changes to welfare benefits announced in the 1998 budget (Rasmussen & Lamm, 2000).

Outcomes: the unfulfilled expectations of stronger productivity growth

One of the well-published purposes of the ECA was to encourage increased national *labour productivity* by combining changes in the labour market with the already started economic reforms.

'By introducing voluntary unionism and changing bargaining procedures it will increase productivity, enhance employment and encourage the sharing of benefits that flow from increased output' (National Party, 1990, p. 27).

However, the Act fell short of these expectations. Although there were many reports of increased productivity within individual organisations, it caused alarm when dismal national labour productivity figures started to appear in the mid-1990s (for an overview of estimates, see Rasmussen, 2009, p. 449).[2] The exact reasons for the low productivity in New Zealand were puzzling and no single obvious explanation was forthcoming. Among the factors being blamed were: inadequate investment in infrastructure (roads, electrical power generation, public transport systems, etc.), insufficient investment in training and education, and lack of positive synergy between the various reforms.

The main reason behind the positive expectations was that it was assumed by proponents of the ECA 1991 that productivity growth was limited by restrictive workplace practices instituted by the award system and union activity. This assumption was even shared by some opponents of the ECA (Easton, 1997, p. 12). As the abolition of the award system and the weakening of union influence did not lead to major productivity increases, other explanations were sought. Instead of union practices, some commentators put the spotlight on the efficiency of management practices in New Zealand (Rasmussen, 2009).

On a theoretical level, the pinpointing of union practices as the culprit for the productivity problems prior to 1990 is in accordance with classical economic models (e.g. Brook, 1990). These models view unions as monopolists who introduce inefficient restrictions on work practices and extract excessive wage increases. The compression of wage differences pursued by many unions is also regarded as damaging to productivity since it can block the efficient allocation of labour – people are not encouraged to shift from low-productivity organisations (paying low wages) to high-productivity organisations (paying high wages).

2. Later analyses of the same period do suggest, however, higher rates. For example, Conway et al. (2015) estimate that labour productivity growth averaged 2.9% in the 1990s, although they attribute a part of the late-1980s and early-1990s growth to labour-shedding associated with the economic reforms and low economic growth (Conway et al., 2015, p. 37).

However, the assumption that union activity always has a negative impact on productivity has been strongly criticised. The counter-attack has underlined the positive effects of union activity (e.g. Freeman & Medoff, 1984). These positive effects can include a reduction in staff turnover because the union is able to make management aware of employee dissatisfaction (the so-called collective or union 'voice'), an upwards pressure on labour costs may induce the employer to implement more efficient labour processes, and union-management collaboration to create more efficient workplace practices can also be very beneficial (Peetz, 1998). This could explain why some countries with a high union density rate, for example the Scandinavian countries, have high productivity levels. Thus, the type of union actions and the setting in which unions operate will often determine the actual impact they have on productivity.

Conclusion

New Zealand's employment relations history is characterised by conflict, conciliation and change. While employment relations began historically with individual bargaining, some individual rights, and traditional employer-employee conflicts, this changed in the 1890s. Then, there was a realisation that conflict could be managed through a formalised conciliation and arbitration system which recognised the collective rights of both employees and employers. The conciliation and arbitration system lasted, with considerable modifications, nearly 100 years. Unsurprisingly, this longevity meant that there were many contextual changes as war, different governments, economic cycles and social pressures all influenced changes to the conciliation and arbitration system. This prompted numerous 'fine tunings' and more substantial changes of the legislative frameworks underpinning the conciliation and arbitration system and, at the end of the 1980s, there had clearly been a considerable shift towards a somewhat different legislative framework.

However, the long reign of the conciliation and arbitration system created a number of ingrained approaches and structures (Rasmussen, 2009, pp. 61-64):

- The legalistic process encouraged an adversarial process;
- The unions' ability to have exclusive bargaining rights through their registrations – and not because of industrial strength – fostered many and weak unions;
- The extension of bargaining outcomes through 'blanket coverage' of industry or occupations meant that many employers were not involved in negotiations;
- Specialised Employment Institutions – for example Conciliation Boards and the Arbitration Court – dealt with negotiations and industrial disputes;
- Individual employment agreements were outside the conciliation and arbitration system and instead they were dealt with under common law jurisdiction;
- Bargaining was restricted to a number of narrowly defined issues ('industrial matters') which limited the demands of the unions and their possible involvement in managerial issues.

Generally, the inability of the conciliation and arbitration system to implement fast and flexible wage adjustments in both upwards and downwards directions was always its weakest point during inflationary and deflationary periods, and this inability became the catalyst for change. The growing focus on pay relativities and the lack of widespread workplace bargaining made the conciliation and arbitration system less suited to an economy integrated into world markets, and this prompted demands for more direct, decentralised bargaining as other parts of the economy was deregulated. Initially, the public sector was leading the way towards decentralised collective bargaining and workplace employment relations. In the private sector, the Labour Relations Act 1987 had less impact than had been expected and this, together with an economic recession, increased the pressure for further change in the 1990s.

The chapter discussed in detail the revolutionary changes facilitated by the ECA. These changes were driven by economic pressures, a different employment relations philosophy and a very different, non-prescriptive legislative framework. This prompted a shift from collective to individual bargaining and towards workplace arrangements. The associated sharp decline in collective bargaining and union density may have been expected, though it also facilitated a high level of individual disputes with personal grievance rights becoming central to employment relations. More surprising (for some) was the disappointing productivity growth and questions arose why this was the case when the supposed culprits of unions, collective agreements and inflexible working practices had much less influence in the 1990s.

In hindsight, the first half of the 1990s marked the high watermark of neo-liberalist, free-market reforms. The general unhappiness with radical reforms prompted a surprising outcome of a 1993 referendum on New Zealand's electoral system with a proportional electoral system (Mixed Member Proportional – MMP) being implemented in the 1996 general election. The radical public sector reforms came under attack from the mid-1990s (especially after the so-called 'Schick Report' in 1996), and were slowly adjusted (Boston, 1999). The ECA 1991 continued to be a controversial, unpopular approach throughout the 1990s. As market-driven, contractual approaches came under attack at the end of the 1990s, the change in government heralded, as will be discussed in the next chapter, another major change in employment relations.

Table 3.2 Historical developments, 1840–1990

Historical developments and events	Reasons for changes/events and consequences
Early Settlers in mid-1800s had good bargaining position	Labour shortages enabled employees to bargain effectively with employers for good wages and working conditions
First employment conflict, involving Parnell in 1840	Disputes over working hours during a time of skilled labour shortages. Parnell won the 8-hour working day (seen as the origin of Labour Day).
Economic depression in late 19th century (1870s to early 1890s)	High unemployment affected working conditions and wages decline. Longer hours were common and boys and girls often worked.
Introduction of Employment of Females Act 1873	This Act was enacted due to public pressure over exploitation of women and children working in factories. However, the Act made no provisions for adequate enforcement and employers often disregarded regulations.
Late 19th century was a time of strong support for trade unions	Reaction to economic depression, exploitation of workers and dire working conditions.
1890 Maritime dispute in Australia that spread to New Zealand. This was the first major national industrial dispute in New Zealand	Arose in Australia over dismissal of union member. Maritime dispute lasted for 56 days. Dispute ended in complete defeat for the participating unions and their supporters. Consequences: employers were able to make non-unionism a condition of work; if employees were found to be in connection with trade unions, they could be dismissed instantly.
Factories Act 1981 and 1894. Right to inspect factories and wage books	The Liberal Government introduced structures of regulated labour market. Legislation designed to protect employment conditions and facilitate wage fixing reform. Factories Act required all factories to be registered. The Act established Department of Labour which had the role of factory inspection.
Industrial Conciliation and Arbitration (IC&A) Act 1894. Act designed to facilitate the settlement of industrial disputes	Influenced by maritime conflict of 1890. Act dealt with strikes and lock-out activity. Sought to protect and promote unions and safeguard the interests of employees. Encouraged formation of industrial and employer associations. Unions gained strength. Features of the Act: · Establishment of conciliation boards · Establishment of Arbitration Court · Registration of unions · No strike clause

1894–1906 no significant strikes	Stability – the IC&A Act seems to work.
1908 Blackball miners' strike. Tension between employers and unions	Poor working conditions in the mine, with main issue being an unreasonable time (15 minutes) for meal breaks. A 3-month strike ends in union victory which changes unions' attitude to IC&A system. Non-registration allows unions to strike and negotiate directly with employers.
Before WW1 in 1914	• Technological advancement • Improved production • Arbitration Court was slow in adjusting wages; 3-yearly reviews insufficient • Unions loose crucial strikes in 1912–13
1920s Economic Downturn	High rate of unemployment and inflation. Decisions handed down by Arbitration Court during this time restricted adjustment of wages and conditions. During the 1920s economic downturn, the Arbitration system weakened
1935 Labour Party in power	Compulsory powers of the Arbitration Court restored. Arbitration Court could also make legal decisions based on social and economic factors rather than just employment. Union membership made compulsory.
1937 Arbitration Court sets minimum wage for women but constitutes only 47% of men's minimum wage	Introduction of the minimum wage was set in line with government policy which maintained that men were heads of household; thus, women were paid considerably less than men.
1951 Waterside dispute	National Party in government after defeat of Labour Government in 1949. Unions unhappy with Arbitration Court progress to settle wage disputes and improve conditions. Employers' refusal to pass on a 15% wage increase granted by Arbitration Court to waterside workers led to longest, costliest and most widespread industrial confrontation in New Zealand history. Lasted 5 months and cost 42 million pounds.
1950s/1960s/1970s recorded an increase in workplace bargaining	Wage settlements under the IC&A system often included additional local agreements (known as 'second tier' agreement). These decentralised pay rises undermined the IC&A system, especially after the infamous 'Nil Decision' by the Arbitration Court was overturned in 1968.

The Industrial Relations Act 1973	'Second tier' agreements based on direct wage bargaining are incorporated into legislative structure.
	Only registered unions could elect to bargain directly with employer and achieve agreements enforceable by courts.
	Industrial Relations Act failed to come to grips with inflationary pressure of the 1970s oil shocks.
Labour Relations Act 1987	Economic and public policy pressures due to international changes in overseas markets (e.g. Britain joining the EU and the 1970s oil crises). Major reforms post-1984: the New Zealand deregulation 'experiment'.
	Employers pressured for deregulated labour market.
	Unions believed that workplace bargaining would result in lower wages and high unemployment rate. This pressure led the Labour Government to introduce the Labour Relations Act 1987.
	Features of the Act included:
	• Mediation Service doing both mediation and conciliation • Act instituted an Arbitration Commission and a Labour Court. • Fundamental change was the introduction of direct bargaining (ability to 'cite out' from award coverage).

Source: Originally developed by Shivashni Priya Singh in 2013; subsequently amended by authors.

References

Alach, P. & Inkson, K. (2004). The new 'Office Temp': Alternative models of contingent labour. *New Zealand Journal of Employment Relations*, *29*(3), 37-52.

Binney, J., Bassett, J. & Olssen, E. (1990). *The people and the land: Te Tangata me Te Whanau*. Allen & Unwin.

Boston, J. (1999). New models of Public Management: the New Zealand case. *Samfundsøkonomen*, 5, 5-15.

Boston, J. & Dalziel, P. (1992). *The Decent Society: Radical Politics in New Zealand*. Oxford University Press.

Brook, P. (1990). *Freedom at Work*. Oxford University Press.

Brook, P. (1991). New Zealand's Employment Contracts Act: An incomplete revolution. *Policy, 7*(3), 12-14.

Brosnan, P. & Walsh, P. (1998). Employment Security in Australia and New Zealand. *Labour & Industry, 8*(3), 23-41.

Burgess, J. & Connell, J. (Eds). (2004). *International Perspectives on Temp Agencies and Workers*. Routledge.

Bush, G. (1995). *Local Government and Politics in New Zealand*. Auckland University Press.

Conway, P., Meehan, L. & Parham, D. (2015). *Who benefits from productivity growth? – The labour income share in New Zealand*. Working Paper 2015/1, NZ Productivity Commission.

Crawford, A., Harbridge, R. & Walsh, P. (2000). Unions and Union Membership in New Zealand: Annual Review for 1999. *New Zealand Journal of Industrial Relations, 25*(3), 291-302.

Dannin, E. (1997). *Working Free: The Origins and Impact of New Zealand's Employment Contracts Act*. Auckland University Press.

Davidson, C., & Bray, M. (1994). *Women and part time work in New Zealand: a contemporary insight*. NZ Institute for Social Research and Development.

Deeks, J., Parker, J. & Ryan, R. (1994). *Labour and Employment Relations in New Zealand*. Longman Paul.

Du Plessis, R. (1993). Women, Politics and the State in New Zealand. In C. Rudd, C. & B. Roper (Eds.), *The Political Economy of New Zealand* (pp. 210-225). Oxford University Press.

Easton, D. (1997). The Economic Impact of the Employment Contracts Act. *Californian Western International Law Journal, 28*(1), 209-220.

Freeman, R. & Medoff, J. (1984). *What Do Unions Do?* Basic Books.

Gilson, C. & Wagar, T. (1997). The Impact of the New Zealand Employment Contracts Act on Individual Contracting: Measuring Organisational Performance. *Californian Western International Law Journal, 28*(1), 221-234.

Grills, W. (1994). The impact of the Employment Contracts Act on the labour law: Implications for unions. *New Zealand Journal of Industrial Relations, 19*(1), 85-101.

Harris, P. & Twiname, L. (1998). *First Knights: an investigation of the New Zealand Business Roundtable*. Howling At The Moon Publishing.

Haworth, N. & Hughes, S. (1995). Under Scrutiny: The ECA, the ILO and the NZCTU Complaint 1993-1995. *New Zealand Journal of Industrial Relations, 20*(2), 143-162.

Holt, J. (1986). *Compulsory arbitration in New Zealand: the First Forty Years*. Auckland University Press.

James, C. (1986). *The quiet revolution: turbulence and transition in contemporary New Zealand*. Allan & Unwin-Port Nicholson Press.

Kelsey, J. (1997). *The New Zealand Experiment: A world model for structural adjustment?* Auckland University Press.

MacDonald, F. (1994, October 8). You're fired, I'm hired: Lawyers are big winners under the Employment Contracts Act. *Listener*, 28-30

McLaughlin, C. (2000). "Mutually Beneficial Agreements" in the Retail Sector? *New Zealand Journal of Industrial Relations, 25*(1), 1-17.

National Party. (1990). *Election Manifesto*.

New Zealand Department of Statistics. (1990). *Labour Market Statistics.* NZ Department of Statistics.

Peetz, D. (1998). *Unions in a Contrary World. The Future of the Australian Trade Union Movement.* Cambridge University Press.

Rasmussen. E. (2009). *Employment Relations in New Zealand.* Pearson.

Rasmussen, E., Bray, M. & Stewart, A. (2019). What is Distinctive about New Zealand's Employment Relations Act 2000?' *Labour & Industry, 29*(1), 52-73.

Rasmussen, E., & Greenwood, G. (2014). Conflict resolution in New Zealand. In W. K. Roche, P. Teague, & A. J. S. Colvin (Eds.), *The Oxford Handbook of Conflict Management in Organizations* (pp. 449-474). Oxford University Press.

Rasmussen, E. & Lamm, F. (2000). 'New Zealand Employment Relations. In G. J Bamber, F. Park, C. Lee, P. K. Ross& K. Broadbent, K. (Eds.), *Employment Relations in the Asia-Pacific: Changing Approaches* (pp. 46-63). Allen & Unwin.

Spicer, B., Emanuel, D. & Powell, M. (1996). *Transforming Government Enterprises: Managing radical organisational change in deregulated environments.* Centre for Independent Studies, Melbourne.

Statistics New Zealand. 1994. *Labour Market 1993.* Statistics New Zealand.

Te Ara Encyclopaedia. (2018). *Story: Strikes and labour disputes.* https://teara.govt.nz/en/strikes-and-labour-disputes/page-10

Walsh, P. (1989). A Family Fight? Industrial Relations Reform under the Fourth Labour Government. In E. Easton (Ed.), *The Making of Rogernomics* (pp. 149-170). Auckland University Press.

Walsh, P. (1993). The State and Industrial Relations in New Zealand. In B. Roper & C. Rudd (Eds.), *State and Economy in New Zealand* (pp. 183-201). Oxford University Press.

Walsh, P. & Ryan, R. (1993). The Making of the Employment Contracts Act. In R. Harbridge (Ed.), *Employment Contracts: New Zealand experiences* (pp. 89-133). Victoria University Press.

Walsh, P. & Wetzel, K. (1993). Preparing for privatisation: Corporate strategy and industrial relations in New Zealand's state owned enterprises. *British Journal of Industrial Relations, 31*(1), 57-74.

Wilson, R. (2000). The decade of non-compliance: The NZ government record of non-compliance with international labour standards 1990-98. *New Zealand Journal of Industrial Relations, 25*(1), 79-94.

4. Employment Relations in the new millennium

ERLING RASMUSSEN; FELICITY LAMM; AND JULIENNE MOLINEAUX

1. To overview the shift in employment relations philosophies from the Employment Contracts Act 1991 to the Employment Relations Act 2000
2. To outline the main employment relations issues and trends in the new millennium
3. To consider the main changes to employment relations processes and outcomes in the 2000s
4. To identify how the 2008–2017 National-led Governments have influenced employment relations outcomes and employment law
5. To speculate on the impact of the post-2017 governments on employment relations

Introduction

The employment relations legislative landscape has undergone significant changes since 2000. This followed the major changes in employment relations under the Employment Contracts Act (ECA) 1991. As anticipated, there was a decline in union density and collective employment contracts in the 1990s. Employees in the secondary labour market also fared less well in the new deregulated labour market.

The critics of such legislative initiatives opposed the free-market philosophy underpinning many of the post-1984 changes and, in particular, they believed that the ECA 1991 engendered a low-skill, low-wage, low-productivity economy. It was unsurprising, therefore, that the newly elected Labour-led Coalition Government set about overhauling several pieces of employment legislation, including employment relations, health and safety and accident compensation, after its election in 1999.

The Employment Relations Act (ERA) 2000 sought to move employment relations from a focus on contractual and market exchanges to one that focused on employment *relationships*. According to its architect, Margaret Wilson, the main goals of the ERA were to promote good faith, collective bargaining and productivity by balancing the power of the parties, promoting trust-based employment relationships and safeguard individual employment rights (Wilson, 2004). However, in the years since the introduction of the ERA, there has been less of a re-balancing of collectivism and individualism, and there are still debates about the efficacy of particular legislative intentions and interventions.

The controversy surrounding the ERA 2000 has continued, and is still continuing, though the longevity of the Act means that some of its key components have become part of mainstream employment relations. We will separate our discussion of legislative changes into three phases: 1) the Labour-led Governments (1999–2008); 2) the National-led Governments (2008–2017); and, 3) the post-2017 Labour-led Governments. As will be shown, there were considerable differences between the employment relations approach of these successive governments, though it is still too early to be definite about the full extent of employment relations interventions in the post-2017 period.

These three political phases have influenced labour market and employment relations outcomes. However, our overview of bargaining outcomes and employment changes will look at the 2000s as a whole. The overview can also be aligned with analyses in Chapter 6 where we address the labour market changes and in particular, the shift towards a knowledge and service economy. These changes have been associated with an increased focus on vocational education and training as there has been considerable pressure to provide suitable trained employees since the late 1990s.

Table 4.1 The shift in employment relations philosophy – 1980s to 2020s

Year	Policy/Philosophy	Outcome
Prior 1984	<ul><li>Keynesian economic policies</li><li>Employment relationship is unique. There is an inherent disparity of power between employers and employees</li><li>Unions are necessary</li><li>Goal: a balance of interests between employers and employees</li></ul>	<ul><li>State regulation and involvement</li><li>Welfare state provisions</li><li>IC&A system</li><li>Collective organisation of employees required</li><li>Awards regulate market & bargaining relations</li><li>Slow drift towards more collective bargaining</li><li>Individual employment agreements dealt with separately</li></ul>
Late 1980s and through 1990s	<ul><li>Free market ideology and belief in market forces to regulate</li><li>Employment relationship no different to any other private contractual relationship between two parties</li><li>Unions impede efficient bargaining exchanges</li><li>Goal: allow for the most efficient bargaining exchanges with state intervention kept to a minimum</li></ul>	<ul><li>The Employment Contracts Act 1991</li><li>Freedom of association</li><li>Employer and employee choice whether to negotiate an individual employment contract or be bound to a collective contract</li><li>Promotion of individual employee rights</li></ul>
The 2000s, allowing for 3 different phases	<ul><li>Post-Keynesian and market-focused economic policies</li><li>Promoting good faith and employment relationships</li><li>Employment relationship is unique. There is an inherent disparity of power between employers and employees</li><li>Unions and collective bargaining are promoted</li><li>Goal: a balance of interests between employers and employees</li><li>Goal: a balance of collective and individual employee interests and protections</li></ul>	<ul><li>The Employment Relations Act 2000, with amendments</li><li>'Productive employment relationships'</li><li>Built on mutual trust and confidence and good faith behaviour and bargaining</li><li>Collective bargaining and ILO principles promoted</li><li>Integrity of individual choice protected</li><li>Mediation as primary step in conflict resolution</li><li>Reduce need for judicial intervention</li></ul>

Source: Developed by authors

Key employment relations debates of the 2000s

As discussed in the previous chapters, ideology plays a crucial part in developing our understandings of employment relations, employment and the labour market. Ideological differences were driving the changes from the IC&A system to the ECA 1991 and other legislative changes in the post-1984 period (see Chapters 3 and 5), and they were also at the fore in employment relations changes in the 2000s (see Table 4.2).

It could be argued that the ERA 2000 has continued the 'two-hands approach' from the 1980s where the move towards more collective and workplace bargaining was re-balanced by more protective measures favouring weaker groups. While the ERA 2000 was seeking to encourage more collective bargaining, it also continued and increased individual employee rights (Rasmussen, 2004; 2010). In other respects, there was a strong overhang of free-market approaches from the 1980s and 1990s, with state interventions often viewed with suspicion, as can be seen by the debates in the 2000s over personal grievance rights and industry- or occupation-based collective bargaining (see below).

While the regulation around collectivism was still an important political issue in the new millennium, it is noticeable that many of the employment relations debates and changes had implications for individual employee rights. It is also noticeable that New Zealand has not returned to the award system (unlike Australia where it continues to play an important role – see Bray et al., 2018). The absence of awards has had considerable impact on employment conditions in many low paying occupations and jobs, and the dispersion of wages and 'living wages' have become constant themes in media and public policy debates (see Chapter 6). Although there have been some attempts to compensate for the absence of awards – for example, the 'living wage' campaign, the tripartite negotiations in the aged-care sector and the proposed Fair Pay Agreements – this is a long way off from both the situations in the 1980s or the current situation in Australia.

The ideological colour of the government has a strong influence on the support of collectivism. The Labour-led Governments have supported more collective bargaining and union activity; for example, this is very explicit in the ERA's Object Clause (see below), while National-led Governments have tried to curtail union activity in various ways. However, the ideological differences have become less pronounced in employment relations in the 2000s. Thus, there are no longer discussions of displacing the ERA (see below), collective bargaining and union activity regulations are only adjusted incrementally, there is broad-based support of most individual employment rights (though maybe not always their particular level), the well-established processes of dispute resolution has continued as has the conflict-solving roles of the Employment Institutions, and the concepts of good faith and individual choice have become embedded (McAndrew et al., 2018). Still, there are some ideological differences and these have come to the fore when there is a change in government or when proposed changes to legislative frameworks are announced (Foster & Rasmussen, 2017; Skilling, 2019).

In the following, we have picked a few examples that illustrate these ideological tensions and how they have played out in debates and their associated outcomes. There were two instances of fierce public debates over employment relations changes during the 2000–2008 Labour-led Governments. When the Labour-led Government announced its intended new legislative framework – the Employment Relations Bill – in early 2000, this prompted a very strong reaction from the political opposition, employer groups and individual employers. While there was an adverse reaction to the legislation's philosophical underpinnings, there were also misgivings about a range of particular issues – from union promotion to good faith and the role of fixed-term agreements and independent contractors. Overall, it was predicted that the legislation would reduce workplace flexibility, increase compliance costs and enhance potential conflict areas (for an overview, see Rasmussen, 2009, pp. 103-106). As political and employer dissatisfaction spilled over into negative business sentiments – the so-called 'winter of discontent' – the Labour-led Government yielded, and the final legislation – the ERA 2000 – included several concessions to the various criticisms.

While the employer campaign subsided significantly after the ERA's enactment – perhaps because many employers found that day-to-day processes and outcomes had not changed that much (see below) – a similar controversy was ignited in 2003–2004 when the amendments to the ERA were proposed. Again, the government took on board some of criticisms and the controversy quickly died down. Although it can be argued, in light of actual changes to processes and outcomes, that the reactions towards the changes were out of proportion, they did, however, highlight different employment relations understandings. It is also suggested that the strong reactions did serve a purpose as the planned legislative changes were watered down. These fundamental differences came to the fore again as a new National-led Government took office in 2008 and prompted further changes to accommodate the concerns of employers.

There were also numerous instances of fierce debate during the National-led Governments 2008–2017. Many of the changes, highlighted in Table 2, were greeted with public protests and union campaigns. These campaigns were similar to the debates under the previous Labour-led Governments in that they were sparked by different ideologies and opposition to particular changes and while the debates were fierce, they also died down rather quickly. Still, the concerns behind the 2008–2017 debates were deep-seated and this explains many of the changes being implemented or foreshadowed by the post-2017 Labour-led Governments (see below).

Interestingly, there were two instances where major public policy changes have had a significant impact of the ERA's longevity and its regulatory impact. First, the National Party decided, prior to the 2008 election, to forego abolishing the ERA and instead took a more piecemeal legislative approach within the overall ERA framework. This made employment relations less of a political issue, though there were still major differences between the two main parties in the subsequent general elections in 2011, 2014, 2017 (Haworth 2011; Rasmussen et al., 2014; Foster & Rasmussen, 2017). Second, concerns about low pay and contractual arrangements and, in particular, health and safety (see Chapter 5) were partly accommodated under the National-led Governments. These legislative adjustments narrowed that gap between the two major parties and highlighted that national employment standards were broadly based political issues (Campbell, 2018).

Although it is too early to say something definite about employment relations under the post-2017 Labour-led Governments, there are already similarities in respect of the nature of debates, compared to the first two phases of the ERA. So far, the post-2017 governments have started – under considerable protests from the National Party and employer groups – to roll back some of the changes implemented under the previous 2008–2017 governments. This is highlighted through the ER Amendment Act 2018 (Skilling, 2019), enhancing statutory minima and pursuing stronger regulatory enforcement. There is also a possibility of more fundamental changes in areas, such as collective bargaining, contracting, statutory minima and pay and employment equity (see below). These areas have been scoped by various working groups, ministerial taskforces and public policy analysts.

However, it is unclear whether they will all be addressed legislatively before the next general election and, if not, whether they may be resurrected subsequently. Thus, there are many unknowns and it is unclear whether we will be witnessing a substantial break with previous public policies.

The three phases of the Employment Relations Act 2000

Phase 1: the Clark Governments, 1999–2008

As mentioned above, the Employment Relations Bill was greeted with fierce employer opposition and dramatic claims about a return to the 'bad old days' of the conciliation and arbitration system. However, this was far from the reality since the Bill continued many of the changes introduced by the ECA 1991 and the final Act had, despite its emphasis on collectivism and 'addressing the inherent inequality of bargaining power', also a strong emphasis on individual employee rights.

Figure 4.1 The object clause of the Employment Relations Act 2000

The object of this Act is –

(a) to build productive employment relationships through the promotion of mutual trust and confidence in all aspects of the employment environment and of the employment relationship –

(i) by recognising that employment relationships must be built on good faith behaviour; and
(ii) by acknowledging and addressing the inherent inequality of bargaining power in employment relationships; and
(iii) by promoting collective bargaining; and
(iv) by protecting the integrity of individual choice; and
(v) by promoting mediation as the primary problem-solving mechanism; and
(vi) by reducing the need for judicial intervention; and

(b) to promote observance in New Zealand of the principles underlying International Labour Organisation Convention 87 on Freedom of Association, and Convention 98 on the Right to Organise and Bargain Collectively.

This is a different Act from the ECA 1991 with its emphasis on 'productive employment relationships', 'addressing the inherent inequality of bargaining power', making good faith an overarching duty, moving the terminology from contracts to agreements, and seeing collectivism as part of the solution (rather than as the problem) of moving towards productive and fair employment relationships. The support of collectivism (collective employment agreements – CEAs) came in several forms, such as:

- Union 'ownership' of collective agreements; thereby disallowing 'collective contracting'
- 30-day rule: new employees join existing CEA
- Unions could initiate bargaining before employers
- Multi-employer CEAs no longer have strike restrictions
- Union registration was re-introduced

However, there was no duty to conclude collective bargaining negotiations, awards were not reinstated, and the conclusion of multi-employer agreements appeared convoluted and difficult in the face of employer resistance. Importantly, the individualistic nature of the ECA 1991 also appeared in several parts of the ERA 2000, and it appeared that the government introduced something like the 'two-handed approach' of the Labour Relations Act 1987 (see Chapter 3). With 'collective contracting' no longer being an option for employers, it was probably a surprise that the expected rise in CEAs in the private sector did not happen. Instead, many of the collective contracts became individual employment agreements (IEAs) to fit with the new regulations.

A comprehensive 2002–2003 analysis of trends under the ERA 2000 found that in most workplaces it was 'business as usual' (Waldegrave et al., 2003; Waldegrave, 2004a & 2004b). There had not been a shift towards collectivism and the vast majority of employees, particularly in small private sector workplaces, were on IEAs. It also appeared that most employers and employees were quite happy with their workplace employment arrangements, though this was not the case for a significant minority of employees where low pay, unsatisfactory working conditions and career prospects fell short of 'productive employment relationships'. Surveys in the late 1990s had found a similar distinction between employee groups (Waldegrave et al., 2003, p. 21) and thus, the aspirations of moving towards a different form of employment relations were unfulfilled.

The Labour Coalition Government reacted by suggesting further legislation which the political opposition and employers greeted, like in 2000, with a strong campaign of criticism and hostility. However, the government went ahead with its changes to support good faith, the promotion of collective bargaining and facilitating union activities and membership (for an overview, see Rasmussen, 2009, pp. 159-163). There were also changes to statutory minimum wages, parental leave and the Holidays Act that ensconced youth statutory minimum wages, paid parental leave (introduced in 2002) and a fourth week of annual leave.

While the legislative changes continued the strong feature of policy-induced changes, especially in terms of statutory minima, there appeared to be very limited impact on bargaining processes and outcomes. The impact of good faith on workplace relationships was unclear and collective bargaining and union membership were stagnant. In fact, there was hardly any progress in moving outside the traditional strongholds of unions in the public sector and larger private sector businesses. This prompted a discussion of why the expected upswing in private sector collective bargaining had not happened (see below).

Besides the strong rise in individual statutory minima – for example, a rise in the adult statutory minimum wage of 59% during 2000–2008 – there was a more buoyant labour market and skill shortages were a major media and policy topic during 2003–2008. There were clear benefits for a large part of the workforce with more job opportunities, higher pay, better working conditions and increased emphasis on employee-friendly flexibility. Skill shortages also prompted a stronger tripartite focus on vocational training and education (see Chapter 6). Still, there was insufficient movement amongst low-paid employee groups and disappointing productivity growth highlighted the concerns about the elusive goal of 'productive employment relationships' (see Chapter 6).

Phase 2: the Key/English Governments, 2008–2017

The fifth National Government was elected in October 2008. The initial years of the National-led Governments were strongly influenced by changing economic circumstances where the Global Financial Crisis shifted labour market settings considerably from a tight labour market with skills shortages to an unpredictable labour market with several OECD countries recording sharp rises in unemployment (Cazes et al., 2013). The crisis feeling was further escalated by the Christchurch earthquakes in 2010–11 which devastated New Zealand's third largest city. While unemployment was contained below 7% in the 2008–2012 period, there were clearly significant economic, labour market and social pressures, including a considerable deterioration of the country's fiscal position as the government borrowed heavily.

Prior to the 2008 election campaign, the new leader of the National Party, John Key, had shifted the National Party's position from abolishing the ERA 2000 to promising specific changes in particular areas. These changes included: a 'probationary' period where new employees could agree to forego their personal grievance rights (subsequently termed the '90-day trial period'), removing the monopoly rights of unions of collective agreements, revisiting the Holidays Act, and removing Accident Compensation Corporation's (ACC) monopoly over workplace insurance costs (Rasmussen & Anderson, 2010).

Interestingly, it appeared that employment relations were not one of the main platform policies for the incoming National-led Government in 2008. It presented its plans as just a tweaking of the legislative frameworks rather than a root-and-branch reform (Haworth, 2011). Although the government quickly introduced the 90-day trial period for small businesses, it was through its subsequent terms in parliament that it made several changes to the ERA and other pieces of employment relations legislations (see Table 4.2).

The changes to personal grievance rights of new employees were clearly a major political point of disagreement and generated both considerable support and opposition. The changes were promoted as 'building flexibility and creating jobs' as well as 'bringing balance to labour market rules' (National Government Employment Relations Policy, 2011). There was strong employer support for the 90-day trial periods and even employers who did not apply trial periods in their own workplaces, were supportive of 'more flexibility' (Foster et al., 2013; Rasmussen et al., 2016). On the other hand, unions were strongly opposed to the undermining of individual personal grievance rights and they campaigned vigorously to have them overturned. This was also the Labour Party's policy in the 2017 General Election but the government decided, in 2018, that smaller businesses (less than 20 employees) could continue to negotiate 90-day trial periods (see below). Thus, this returned the employee personal grievance rights to the situation before the 2010 changes (see Table 2).

There was considerable debate over the effectiveness of the 90-day trial periods. Most the research by the Ministry of Business, Innovation and Employment (MBIE) was focused on employers and their approaches. Subsequently, MBIE developed a very comprehensive survey of employers – the National Employer Survey – which so far has recorded annually the opinions and work practices of employers since 2015 (MBIE, 2019). The MBIE surveys, together with several surveys conducted by employer associations, clearly found that employers were in favour of the 90-day trial periods. These sentiments were also mirrored in independent surveys (see Foster et al., 2013).

Table 4.2 Major employment relations policy changes 2008–2017

Legislation	Legislative purpose and details
ER Amendment Act 2008	Introduce 90-day probation/trial period for small businesses (1 to 19 employees)
ER Amendment Act 2010	Extend 90-day trial period to all organisations, reduced union access rights, reinstatement is no longer primary remedy in dismissal cases, change dismissal test from what a reasonable employer 'would' instead of 'could' have done
Holidays Amendment Act 2010	Employers can require proof of sickness from the first day, allow employees to trade for cash their fourth week of annual leave
ER (Film Production Work) Amendment Act 2010	'Hobbit' legislation prescribes 'contracting' for film production workers
ER (Secret Ballots for Strikes) Amendment Act 2012	Before taking strike action, unions need to conduct secret ballots of members
ER Amendment Bill 2013 (implemented after the 2014 General Election)	Changes good faith duty to conclude collective bargaining, allow opting out of multi-employer agreement bargaining, meal and refreshment breaks can be removed, allow pay reduction for partial strikes, changes transfer regulation (Part 6A), strike notice requirements changed
Minimum Wage (Starting-out Wage) Amendment Act 2013	Reduce starting-out wages for 16-19 years employees to 80% of adult statutory minimum wage (applies only to 18-19 years olds if they have been on benefit prior to starting job)
Health and Safety legislation	The Health and Safety Reform Bill in March 2014 extends the duty of care to all persons in control of a business or undertaking, worker participation is strengthened. New enforcement agency Worksafe NZ is created. The Accident Compensation Act underwent two amendments in 2008 and 2010. The amendments were primarily concerned with reducing the number of claims and associated costs.
ER Amendment Act 2016 (Employment Standards)	Increased Parental Leave to 18 weeks. 'Zero hours' restricted by preventing employers altering shifts at short notice and guaranteeing minimum number of hours. Increasing recording obligations (wage and hours) for employers and more regulatory powers of Labour Inspectors.

Source: Foster & Rasmussen, 2017, p.102

While there was no doubt that employers generally agreed to the 90-day trial period and that unions were strongly opposed to it, there was less clarity about the impact on employees and associated employment effects. The government argued that many people continued their employment past the 90 days and that a 'hassle-free' trial period created many additional jobs. However, 2016 research by economic research institute, Motu, found very limited or no employment effects: 'We find no evidence that the ability to use trial periods increases firms' overall hiring; /... / We also find no evidence that the policy increased the probability that a new hire by a firm was a disadvantaged jobseeker...' (Chappell & Sin, 2016, pp. i-ii). Thus, the jury is still out regarding positive or negative effects, though it is obvious that this is an intervention that divides the main political parties (see below).

The National Party had promised in the 2008 election that it would revisit the Holidays Act. This resulted in the specific changes which allow employees to 'trade in' their fourth week of holiday for cash. However, a major overhaul of the Holidays Act did not happen and its application could often be problematic for employers and generated a fair amount of disagreement between employers and employees. There have also been several cases where employers have deliberately withheld holiday payments (see below). A major overhaul of the Holidays Act is still on the agenda and the 2017 Labour-led Government tasked a working group to come up with suitable recommendations which prompted subsequently a legislative amendment scheduled for 2022.

Interestingly, the ability to 'trade in' a week of annual leave had already been suggested by the National-led Government in 1998 (Rasmussen & Anderson, 2010, p. 220) but it was never implemented. This would have been a more significant shift in practice as annual leave at that time was still three weeks and was not increased until 2007. Likewise, the election promise of removing ACC's monopoly over workplace insurance costs was also a resurrection of a policy of the 1990s where the National-led Government implemented such a change in 1998, which was subsequently overturned by the Labour-led Government in 2001 (see Chapter 5). Despite some government and business criticism of ACC over its levies and bureaucratic structure during the 2008–2017 period, there was never any legislative appetite to abolish ACC's workplace insurance role as it fulfilled several functions, including compensation, rehabilitation and prevention.

Although there was a strong focus on adjusting individual employee rights during 2008–2017, there was also a number of changes to the role of unions and collective bargaining (see Table 4.2). These changes happened in several stages. In 2010, the unions' right of access to workplaces was curtailed with employer consent necessary before unions could enter workplaces and discuss union matters with employees. In 2012, unions' ability to take strike action was constrained as they had to conduct secret ballots of their members before taking action. In 2014, there were changes to bargaining processes of multi-employer agreements which allowed employers to stall and avoid negotiations over multi-employer agreements. There were also changes to unions' ability to take strike action with tougher notice requirements and employer ability to deduct pay over partial strikes. These changes – and other minor regulatory changes – made it more difficult for unions to conduct collective bargaining and it is difficult to see how the changes aligned with the ERA's Objectives and their emphasis on promoting collective bargaining.

A particular intervention against unionism and collective bargaining was the so-called 'Hobbit' law changes in the film production industry (see the detailed discussion in *New Zealand Journal of Employment Relations,* 36(3)). As highlighted in the detailed discussion below, it was triggered by a collective bargaining dispute, but its prior history related to legal court cases over the employment status – contractor or employee – of a worker at the film company, Three Foot Under, associated with filmmaker, Peter Jackson. A government legislative intervention designated all film production workers as contractors where both the content and processes surrounding the intervention made this a controversial public policy change.

In conclusion, the changes to employment relations that occurred under the National-led Governments were aimed at enhancing labour market flexibility and employers' ease of conducting business. The changes were initially driven by the fear of a strong rise in unemployment and business failures as the Global Financial Crisis put major pressure on labour markets in most OECD countries. It also aimed, as discussed in Chapter 6, at improving workplace productivity and thus, according to Department of Labour, '...the changes are aimed at creating a more flexible and responsive labour market, which in turn is expected to contribute indirectly to improved productivity in a number of sectors' (Department of Labour, 2010, p. 5).

However, as the pressure from the Global Financial Crisis eased, a less clear-cut public policy pattern developed during 2013-2017. On one hand, the search for 'a more flexible and responsive labour market' and the promotion of more individualised employment relations continued as reflected in the Employment Relations Amendment Act 2014. On the other hand, the growing concerns about employment conditions and their corresponding social impact resulted in the National-led Government implementing further employment regulation and highlighting the importance of employment standards (see Table 4.2).

Phase 3: The initial years of the Ardern Governments, 2017-onwards

The 2017 General Election was a close fought battle and included two new party leaders, with Bill English becoming Prime Minister and leader of the National Party when Prime Minister John Key resigned in December 2016, and Jacinta Ardern becoming leader of the Labour Party in August 2017. As a coalition government was the likely election outcome, there was also an interest in the minor parties' election manifestos (Skilling & Molineaux, 2017). After the Labour Party and New Zealand First reached a coalition agreement, a coalition government with Labour and New Zealand First, and with the support of the Green Party, was formed in October 2017.

It was obvious from their election manifestos that the Labour Party-New Zealand First coalition agreement and subsequent policy announcements would herald a significant change to existing employment relations (Coalition Agreement, 2017; Foster & Rasmussen, 2017). This included a reversal of changes implemented in 2008–2017 and new initiatives to enhance collectivism, employee protection and promote fairness and equality in the labour market. These significant changes included: large annual increases in the statutory minimum wage towards the goal of $20 by early 2021, an increase in paid parental leave from 22 to 26 weeks from July 2020, and the promotion of a 'living wage' for public sector employees. An interesting development was the Equal Pay Amendment Act which came into force in November 2020. It has been suggested that this Act could cause an upheaval of pay structures, given the already considerable impact of the pay equity changes in the aged-care sector.

As can be seen from Table 4.3, the Employment Relations Amendment Act 2018 reversed several of the 2008–2017 interventions. It is surprising that the Labour Coalition Government did not abolish totally the 90-day trial periods, but these can still be pursued by small businesses with less than 20 employees. This reversal brings back the 2010 situation, instead of the pre-December 2008 situation where all employees had a personal grievance right. While there were some initiatives to promote union membership, it is still too early to say whether it will overcome the stagnation in union density.

Although there have been several changes post-2017, there are still many more changes which could prove significant as the 2017–2020 government launched several working groups, legislative reviews and expert discussions. This has included working groups on Fair Pay Agreements, the so-called 'Hobbit' legislation about contractors in the film production industry, the link between social welfare and employment, and a review of the Holidays Act. A major restructuring of vocational education and training was announced in 2019 and is under implementation in 2020–2021 (see Chapter 6).

Table 4.3 Major provisions of the ER Amendment Act (2018)

Changes in effect from 12 December 2018	Changes in effect from 6 May 2019
Union representatives can now enter workplaces without consent, provided the employees are covered under, or bargaining towards, a collective agreement	The right to set the number and duration of rest and meal breaks will be restored
Pay deductions can no longer be made for partial strikes	90-day trial periods will be restricted to businesses with less than 20 employees
Businesses must now enter into bargaining for multi-employer collective agreements, if asked to join by a union	Employees in specified 'vulnerable industries' will be able to transfer on their current terms and conditions in their employment agreement if their work is restructured, regardless of the size of their employer
Employees will have extended protections against discrimination on the basis of their union membership status	The duty to conclude bargaining will be restored for single-employer collective bargaining
If requested by the employee, reinstatement will be the first course of action considered by the Employment Relations Authority	For the first 30 days of their employment, new employees must be employed under terms consistent with the collective agreement
Earlier initiation timeframes have been restored for unions in collective bargaining	Pay rates will need to be included in collective agreements
New categories of employees may apply to receive the protections afforded to 'vulnerable employees'	Employers will need to provide new employees with an approved active choice form within the first 10 days of employment and return forms to the applicable union
	Employers will need to allow for reasonable paid time for union delegates to undertake their union activities
	Employees will need to pass on information about the role and function of unions to prospective employees

Source: Skilling, 2019, p. 64

As various changes are still unfolding or being discussed, it is difficult to make a precise evaluation of the employment relations policies of both the 2017–2020 coalition government and the current Labour Government. With the 2020 General Election resulting in a majority

Labour Government, it appears likely that many policy recommendations could be phased in during 2021–2023.

Overall, the changes are more in line with the ERA's object clause and policy intentions (compared to the 2008–2017 changes), though whether they will deliver on establishing more 'productive employment relationships' and promoting collectivism are still unclear. Furthermore, the economic, social and labour market upheavals resulting from the Covid-19 pandemic make it even more difficult to predict public policy changes in employment relations (see Chapter 6). Several major industries – for example, tourism, hospitality and retail – have recorded significant employment losses and they will take considerable time to overcome the current downturn as a result of the Covid-19 restrictions. While a major effort in vocational training and education has been signalled, it is unclear how the government will prioritise new regulatory interventions, including support of low-paid employees.

Unions, bargaining outcomes and labour market changes

As mentioned, the ERA supported explicitly collectivism and positioned it as part of the solution – rather than a barrier – in moving towards 'productive employment relationships'. Despite several positive interventions in the ERA to support collectivism, it is clear from Table 4.4 below that the legislative intentions have not translated into union membership growth. In fact, the union density figures – as a percentage of employees – hide a decline in private sector unionism under the ERA: union density is still high in the public sector with around 60% being union members while union density has hovered around or below 10% in the private sector in recent years. Thus, there are many private sector workplaces where union activity is very limited or non-existent.

Table 4.4 Unions, union membership and union density

Month	Year	Number of unions	Membership	Density (%)
September	1989	112	648 825	44.7
May	1991	80	603 118	41.5
December	1991	66	514 325	35.4
December	1995	82	362 200	21.7
December	1999	82	302 405	17.0
December	2000	134	318 519	21.6
December	2004	170	354 058	21.1
December	2008	147	384 777	21.4
December	2011	134	372 891	20.5
December	2014	125	361 491	18.5
March	2017	124	355 511	17.2

Sources: Ryall & Blumenfeld, 2015; Companies Office, 2018

Since the start of the ERA, there has been a rise in the number of new and larger unions, often as a result of amalgamations, for example, E tū. One of the reasons for the creation of new unions is the 'ownership' of collective agreements by certain unions (Barry & May, 2004; Murrie, 2006). Recruiting new, younger members to replace retired workers in relatively stable employment is also problematic, as shown in the graphs below. Some younger workers can be changing jobs often, being precariously employed and holding down multiple jobs, thus making union recruitment difficult. Additionally, the prevalence of small businesses is clearly a problem for effective union organising and so are sectors with high staff turnover with union recruitment of new members being a constant, ongoing task. Still, it has probably surprised some commentators that unions have had so little success under a positive legislative framework.

Figure 4.2 Union membership

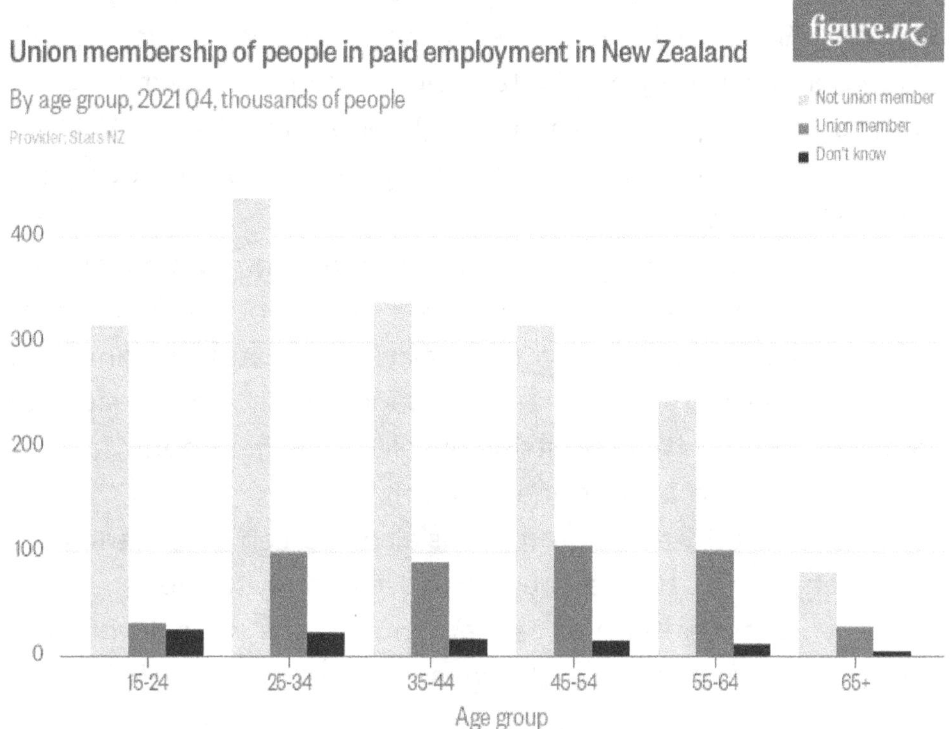

Why have unions not been more successful in growing membership and lifting union density under the ERA? There are numerous factors and explanations in play and many of them have been mentioned in the debate (for an overview, see Rasmussen, 2009, pp. 129-133):

- Many private sector workplaces are not conducive to effective union organising because of factors such as their size and their high staff turnover. This is often linked to the 'presentation gap' concept where employees may want to become union members but they have little or no option as union activity does not cover their workplace.
- The so-called 'passing on' of union negotiated benefits featured strongly in the debate of the early 2000s and was sought to be addressed by the ER Amendment Act 2004. However, many employers like to have similar pay and conditions across their

workforce, and this makes 'passing on' a normal practice.

- 'Free-loading' or 'free-riding' have been a traditional argument (Olson, 1980; Crouch, 1982) where employees decide against union membership as they may obtain the same or nearly similar pay and conditions as union members (Waldegrave et al., 2003, pp.76-77). The existence of 'passing on' will encourage such an employee decision.
- The growth in individual employment rights and minima and a buoyant labour market have also been mentioned as a problem (Rasmussen et al., 2006). With a sharp rise in statutory minima and employers facing skill and staff shortages, many employees have received improvements outside of collective agreements (aligned with points 1 and 3 mentioned above).
- Employee apathy or disinterest has also been an argument since many employees have expressed satisfaction with their employment relationships or they would prefer to deal with any dissatisfaction themselves (Haynes et al., 2006).
- Employers' negative attitudes towards collective bargaining or reluctance to enter into collective bargaining have been seen as a major stumbling block, whether or not a particular employer has actively resisted collective bargaining taking place.

Research has indicated that the latter point has some validity since employers tend to have negative attitudes towards collective bargaining (Foster et al., 2009 & 2011; Geare et al., 2006 & 2009). This was obvious in the ferocious employer criticism of the ERA 2000 and its Amendment Act in 2004. While the intensity of this employer criticism reduced over time, there was a running criticism of various parts of the ERA 2000 and the 'inconvenience' caused to employers (Burton, 2004 & 2010). Surveys and interviews conducted in 2008–2010 found that there were two distinct groups of employers. 'Of those engaged in collective bargaining, only 21% believed their employees lacked interest in the process. Of those not engaged, the proportion is reversed with 70.1% arguing their employees lacked any form of interest in collective bargaining' (Foster et al., 2011, p. 201). Likewise, it was found that many employers supported the constraints on union activity imposed during the 2008–2017 National-led Governments (Foster et al., 2013; Rasmussen, et al., 2016).

Thus, unions have had limited success in extending collective bargaining coverage in the post-2000 period (Blumenfeld & Donnelly, 2017). Public sector collective bargaining coverage has been solid and has increased from the ECA 1991 period (in fact, it has increased since 1995). The large, homogenous public sector workforce – for example, in education, health and core public sector – provides an easier workforce to organise for unions. There is also often an overlap between collective bargaining and occupational identity; something evident in recent public sector disputes. However, the lower number of employees in the public sector – around 6 times smaller than the private sector workforce – means that the overall collective bargaining coverage is dragged down by the drop in private sector collective bargaining.

The link between collective bargaining coverage and union membership has been strong under the ERA 2000 with 'collective contracting' not being an option. It is necessary, therefore, for unions to find a way of *both* enhancing private sector collective bargaining and increase private sector union density. This has been addressed by union leaders previously (Harré, 2010; Kelly, 2010) and there are some union expectations that recent ERA amendments, Fair Pay Agreements and other supports of collective bargaining may be able to enhance the unions' membership initiatives. As the final form of the current government's employment relations policies has yet to be established, and as many of the structural and embedded barriers (as discussed above) are still in evidence, a turnaround in union density and membership and collective bargaining coverage is highly unpredictable.

Employment law under the Employment Relations Act

Under the ERA 2000, there have been several high-profile court decisions (though less pronounced compared to the 1990s). There have been some links between legislative interventions and court decisions in a couple of key areas, such as employment status (the Bryson case), pay equity (the Bartlett case), employment standards, and collective bargaining. Court decisions have provided clarification on a number of issues, such as availability to work overtime, payment for rest breaks and meetings, redeployment in organisational restructuring (Kiely, 2018; 2019). However, the fundamental political disagreements surrounding the ERA 2000 – see the 3 phases described above – have also left a number of issues to be re-litigated, unresolved or bypassed in silence. Amongst these issues are the Holidays Act, employment status (particularly involving rights and protection of contractors), pay equity and employment standards.

The employment status of workers – whether they are employees or contractors – has been tested in several court cases, with the decisions in the so-called Bryson case playing a major role. The case between Mr Bryson, working on the Lord of the Rings film series, and Peter Jackson's production company, Three Foot Six Limited, was tested at the Employment Court, the Court of Appeal and finally at the Supreme Court (see Nuttall & Reid, 2005; Rasmussen, 2009, pp. 378-9). The final outcome was that Mr Bryson was considered an employee and he was covered, therefore, by statutory employee rights. The case sends a strong message to employers that they should consider the actual relationship with a worker; just labelling a worker a contractor was insufficient. For workers in the film production industry, this changed with 'Hobbit' legislation in 2010 where workers in that industry were deemed to be contractors (see *New Zealand Journal of Employment Relations*, 36(3)). This controversial legislation is still under consideration as is the legal decision-making on workers' employment status, with new legislative initiatives expected in 2022.

As shown above, unions have not gained traction under the ERA 2000. It can be argued that a number of court decisions have hampered unions' ability to bargain for multi-employer agreements (MECAs), to resist employers' attempt to bypass unions in negotiations, and to break bargaining deadlocks. Employers have been successful in arguing that they should not be forced into a MECA against their wishes. This has proven, besides the cumbersome rules surrounding MECA negotiations, to be a nearly impossible hurdle for the unions to overcome. There have been several court cases dealing with employers attempting to bypass unions during bargaining, either through proposing individual employment agreements or communicating directly with employees. While unions have succeeded in curtailing some employer behaviours, it has proved difficult to avoid direct communication and the lure of individual employment agreements. Finally, the introduction of facilitation as a new approach in the ER Amendment Act 2004 has also had less than expected impact (see Scott, 2019). The outcome from early cases in front of the Employment Relations Authority signalled a very high threshold before the Authority would apply facilitation: lengthy unresolved negotiations and even industrial disputes were not seen as being sufficient. Therefore, there have been very few cases accepted for facilitation since this new dispute resolution method was introduced in 2004.

While unions have been faced with some adverse court decisions, they have also had important wins. In the famous Bartlett or Terranova case, the Service and Food Workers Union pursued the pay equity claim of Kristine Bartlett which was finally upheld when the Court of Appeal supported the previous Employment Court decision. As this decision would have opened for many other court cases, the government decided – following recommendations from a tripartite working group – to underwrite a substantial pay rise for over 50,000 care workers by implementing a $2 billion package in July 2017.

Another key win, the Employment Standards Act 2016, was mainly driven by concerns raised by union campaigns (targeting the unfairness of 'zero hours' agreements) though there were also a number of court cases which highlighted unsatisfactory employment standards. In particular, the Employment Institutions have started to impose severe fines on employers who exploit vulnerable workers, and there are now more labour inspectors and a more proactive approach to enforce employment standards.

Beyond legal precedent, the Employment Institutions have also been very active and dealt with a large number of cases. The Mediation Service is dealing with over 15,000 disputes a year: in 2018, over 8,000 cases were heard by the Mediation Service, and it also signed off on another 8,000 plus settlements concluded directly by the parties themselves (Franks, 2018). The Employment Relations Authority and the Employment Court have also been kept busy, and their cases are often setting or adjusting legal precedent. Still, there are concerns that there are barriers to conflict resolution which prevent some workers and employers to pursue their employment relationship problems. These barriers are often associated with the ERA's expectation that employees have the ability and the inclination to pursue employment relations problems either at the workplace or at the Employment Institutions. This can be an unrealistic expectation since there can be many reasons why employees may not pursue their rights. Instead, many of these employees can opt to keep silent or just leave the workplace.

Conclusion

The ERA 2000 was envisaged as a major break from previous employment legislation, setting the scene for more relational, trust-based employment relationships. As the Act has been in force for two decades, its longevity means that many practitioners have just a dim view of previous employment relations approaches. However, the ECA 1991 is still casting its long shadow over employment relations practices and some of the expectations of more collective bargaining, higher union membership and 'productive employment relationships' have not been fulfilled. Importantly, the controversial status of employment relations legislation is still lingering on and has come to the fore when general elections and major changes occur.

While the main original parts of the ERA 2000 are still intact, there have been many amendments in the post-2000 period. The three phases presented in this chapter show a distinct difference in the various governments' support of the ERA's objectives. Although the Labour-led Governments in 2000–2008 and post-2017 have been active in supporting the objectives of collectivism and improved employee protection, there were more mixed signals under the 2008–2017 National-led Governments. While collective bargaining has stagnated, there has been a strengthening of individual employment rights, and these rights, including the personal grievance right, have now become embedded in New Zealand employment relations.

The political struggles over the particular changes to the ERA 2000 as well as the realities of the changing nature of work will probably be debated for a while and this will make employment relations less consensual and stable. In this environment, it is unclear how well the wider concerns of low productivity growth, insufficient training and skill development, a fragmented labour market and an associated low wage economy can be addressed. There are also conflicts over the appropriate level and forms of labour market *flexibility* where employer demands for further increases in employer discretion is confronted by worker demands of improved protections and flexible working arrangements. Finally, these concerns and conflicts have yet to be influenced by the expected major upheaval associated with the 'future of work' and radical shifts in work and employment patterns, and this could prompt a range of new challenges for employment relations regulations (see Chapter 6).

References

Barry, M. & May, R. (2004). New employee representation: Legal development and New Zealand unions. *Employee Relations*, 26(2), 203-223.

Blumenfeld, S. & Donnelly, N. 2017. Collective Bargaining Across Four Decades: Lessons from CLEW's Collective Agreement Database. In Anderson, G. et al. (eds.), *Transforming Workplace Relations in New Zealand 1976-2016* (pp. 107-128). Victoria University Press.

Bray, M., Waring, P., Cooper, R. & Macneil, J. (2018). *Employment Relations. Theory and Practice*. 4th Edition, McGraw-Hill Education.

Burton, B. (2004). The Employment Relations Act according to Business New Zealand. In Rasmussen, E. (Ed.). *Employment relationships: New Zealand's Employment Relations Act* (pp. 134-144). Auckland University Press.

Burton, B. (2010). Employment relations 2000–2008: an employer view. In Rasmussen, E. (Ed.). *Employment relationships: workers, unions and employers in New Zealand* (pp. 94-115). Auckland University Press.

Campbell, I. (2018). Zero-hour work arrangements in New Zealand: Union action, public controversy and two regulatory initiatives. In O'Sullivan, M., Lavelle,, J., McMahon, J., Ryan, L., Murphy, C., Turner, T. & Gunnigle, P. (Eds.). *Zero Hours and On-call Work in Anglo-Saxon Countries* (pp. 91-110). Springer.

Cazes, S., Verick, S. & Al Hussami, F. (2013). Why did unemployment respond so differently to the global financial crisis across countries? *IZA Journal of Labour Policy*, 2(10), 1-18.

Chappell, N. & Sin, I. (2016). *The Effect of Trial Periods in Employment on Firm Hiring Behaviour*. New Zealand Treasury Working Paper 16/03, June 2016, NZ Treasury.

Coalition Agreement. (2017). *Coalition Agreement New Zealand Labour Party and New Zealand First.* October 2917, NZ Parliament.

Companies Office. (2018). *Union membership return report 2018.* Downloaded from: www.companiesoffice.govt.nz on 17 November 2019.

Crouch, C. (1982). *Trade Unions: the Logic of Collective Action.* Fontana.

Department of Labour. (2010). *Annual Report 2010.* Department of Labour.

Foster, B., Murrie, J. & Laird, I. (2009). It Takes Two to Tango: Evidence of a Decline in Institutional Industrial Relations in New Zealand. *Employee Relations,* 31(5), 503-514.

Foster, B., Rasmussen, E., Laird, I., & Murrie, J. (2011). Supportive legislation, unsupportive employers and collective bargaining in New Zealand. *Relations Industrielles/Industrial Relations,* 66(2), 192-212.

Foster, B., Rasmussen, E. & Coetzee, D. (2013). Ideology versus reality: New Zealand employer attitudes to legislative change of employment relations. *New Zealand Journal of Employment Relations,* 37(3), 50-64.

Foster, B. & Rasmussen, E. (2017). The major parties: National's and Labour's employment relations policies. *New Zealand Journal of Employment Relations,* 42(2), 95-109.

Franks, P. (2018). *Barriers to participation: a mediator's perspective.* Paper at AUT Symposium, see: www.workresearch.aut.ac.nz .

Geare, A., Edgar, F. & McAndrew, I. (2006). Employment Relations: Ideology and HRM Practice. *International Journal of Human Resource Management,* 17(7), 1190-1208.

Geare, A., Edgar, F. & McAndrew, I. (2009). Workplace Values and Beliefs: An Empirical Study of Ideology, High Commitment and Unionisation. *International Journal of Human Resource Management,* 20(5), 1146–1171.

Harré, L. (2010). Collective bargaining – right or privilege? In Rasmussen, E. (Ed.). *Employment relationships: workers, unions and employers in New Zealand* (pp. 24-39). Auckland University Press.

Haworth, N. (2011). A Commentary on Politics and Employment Relations in New Zealand: 2008–2011. *New Zealand Journal of Employment Relations*, 36(2), 23-32.

Haynes, P., Boxall, P. & Macky, K. (2006). Union reach, the 'representation gap' and the prospects for unionism in New Zealand. *Journal of Industrial Relations*, 48(2), 193-216.

Kelly, H. (2010). Challenges and opportunities in New Zealand employment relations: a CTU perspective. In Rasmussen, E. (Ed.). *Employment relationships: workers, unions and employers in New Zealand* (pp. 133-148). Auckland University Press.

MBIE. (2019). *National Survey of Employers 2017/18*. Ministry of Business, Innovation and Employment.

McAndrew, I., Edgar, F. & Jarrard, M. (2018). Human Resource Management and Employment Relations Paradigms in Australia and New Zealand. In Parker, J. & Baird, M. (Eds.). *The Big Issues in Employment* (pp. 1-19). Wolters Kluwer.

Murrie, J. (2006). Not a typical union but a union all the same: New unions under the Employment Relations Act 2000. *New Zealand Journal of Employment Relations*, 31(2), 31-45.

Nuttall, P. & Reid, F. (2005). Three Foot Six Limited v Bryson CA 246/03 12 November 2004 – legal comment. *New Zealand Journal of Employment Relations*, 30(1), 87-92.

Olson, M. (1980). *The Logic of Collective Action*. Harvard University Press.

Rasmussen, E. (2009). *Employment Relations in New Zealand*. Pearson.

Rasmussen, E. (Ed.). (2004). *Employment relationships: New Zealand's Employment Relations Act*. Auckland University Press.

Rasmussen, E. (Ed.). (2010). *Employment relationships: workers, unions and employers in New Zealand*. Auckland University Press.

Rasmussen, E. & Anderson, D. (2010). Between unfinished business and an uncertain future. In Rasmussen, E. (Ed.). *Employment Relationships. Workers, Unions and Employers in New Zealand* (pp. 208-223). Auckland University Press.

Rasmussen, E., Hunt, V. & Lamm, F. (2006). Between individualism and social democracy. *Labour & Industry*, 17(1), 19-40.

Rasmussen, E., Fletcher, M., & Hannam, B. (2014). The major parties: National's and Labour's employment relations policies. *New Zealand Journal of Employment Relations*, 39(1), 21-32.

Rasmussen, E., Foster, B. & Farr, D. (2016). The battle over employer-determined flexibility: attitudes amongst New Zealand employers. *Employee Relations*, 38(6), 1-23.

Ryall & Blumenfeld, S. (2015). *Union and Union Membership in New Zealand – Report on 2015 Survey*. Victoria University.

Scott, J. (2019). *Mediation and Facilitation of Collective Employment Disputes in New Zealand from a Historical and Comparative Perspective*. MPhil Thesis, Auckland University of Technology.

Skilling, P. (2019). Another swing of the pendulum: rhetoric and argument around the Employment Relations Amendment Act (2018). *New Zealand Journal of Employment Relations*, 44(1), 110-128.

Skilling, P. & Molineaux, J. (2017). New Zealand's minor parties and ER policy after 2017. *New Zealand Journal of Employment Relations*, 42(2), 110-128.

Waldegrave, T. (2004a). Employment relationship management under the Employment Relations Act. In Rasmussen, E. (Ed.). *Employment relationships: New Zealand's Employment Relations Act* (pp. 119-133). Auckland University Press.

Waldegrave, T. (2004b). Employee experience of employment relationships under the Employment Relations Act. In Rasmussen, E. (Ed.). *Employment relationships: New Zealand's Employment Relations Act* (pp. 145-158). Auckland University Press.

Waldegrave, T., Anderson, D. & Wong, K. (2003). *Evaluation of the short term impacts of the Employment Relations 2000.* Department of Labour.

Wilson, M. (2004). The Employment Relations Act: a framework for a fairer way. In Rasmussen, E. (Ed.). *Employment relationships: New Zealand's Employment Relations Act* (pp. 9-20). Auckland University Press.

5. The legislative support structure

FELICITY LAMM; ERLING RASMUSSEN; AND JULIENNE MOLINEAUX

1. To present employment laws covering health and safety, privacy and human rights
2. To highlight the debates that surround regulatory and self-regulatory approaches
3. To describe the developments that led to the current protective employment legislation
4. To outline the key principles of and duties under each of the featured laws

Introduction

While the Employment Relations Act provides the foundation for New Zealand's employment law, the Health and Safety at Work Act, the Human Rights Act and the Privacy Act operate as its support structure. For employees, these statutes represent a legislative safety net that sets out minimum enforceable standards. From the point of view of employers, the laws enhance management practices and complement national and international quality, trade and labour standards. The Acts are often seen as a barometer of government employment policy and, in the case of the health and safety legislation, have been used as a precursor of fundamental reforms in employment policy and law – as happened in 1891 and 1988. In these instances, health and safety legislation signalled a shift in government policy from self-regulation to regulation and back again to self-regulation.

Seen as providing some of the basic rights to cover working conditions, privacy and discrimination, the three pieces of legislation have incorporated elements from similar overseas laws and international labour conventions. In order to avoid becoming overly complex, each Act sets out broad principles of compliance in an attempt to cover a wide range of contingencies. Individually, they represent powerful statues with significant penalties and compensatory remedies. For example, the maximum fine available under the Health and Safety at Work Act 2015 is generally $1,500,000 for a company or $300,000 for an individual., with prison terms possible for very serious offending.

In this chapter we provide an overview of the development of the Acts as well as a brief summary of the main principles contained in each statute. This is followed by a discussion highlighting some of the issues surrounding the Acts, such as the rise in the number of discrimination complaints and the reasons why this as occurred.

Occupational Health and Safety

Background

In New Zealand, occupational health and safety has been treated, for many years, as a matter subject to legal intervention. Originating with a specific concern for the protection of workers in the place of work, over the years efforts to control occupational health and safety by law had become piecemeal, complex and unwieldy. The 1970s saw many overseas countries review their occupational health and safety legislation. A notable example was the United Kingdom's Lord Robens' report (1972) on the safety and health at work which outlined the principle of *one Act, administered by one regulatory authority, covering all workers.* While the Robens' Report has had a considerable influence in New Zealand – particularly its recommendation for more joint self-regulation by employers and employees – New Zealand directed its attention to a comprehensive 'no-fault' system of compensation in the case of industrial injury and disease (see the Accident Compensation Act 1972 and 2001, and the Accident Rehabilitation and Compensation Insurance Act 1992).

It was not until 1992 that a Robens-type occupational health and safety legislation was enacted in New Zealand. The Health and Safety in Employment Act 1992 (HASIE Act) was introduced as part of the National Government's employment package. It was intended to reflect the Government's hands-off approach to employment relations and began the process of rationalising occupational health and safety; that is, creating one Act administered by one regulatory authority. It embodied the part of the Robens model whereby state-imposed standards have been developed into performance standards (Campbell, 1992; Lamm, Rasmussen & Anderson, 2013).

The scope of the HASIE Act was broader than that of the previous legislation, which covered only private-sector businesses and identified workplaces by the kind of work carried out or by machinery or processes used. The Act included most employers (whether or not they are principals, self-employed, or control the place of work), and covered most places of work. It has also shifted the legislative emphasis away from the control of specific hazards *to the promotion of risk management* in relation to work activities. The onus was (and still is) entirely on the employer (and to a lesser extent on the employee) to ensure that they create a healthy and safe workplace, with the regulatory agency stepping in only once a breach has occurred.

The failures of the Health and Safety Legislation

Unlike previous occupational health and safety legislation which was more prescriptive, the Health and Safety in Employment Act 1992, set out general duties for employers and employees and was supported by regulations and codes of practices which relate to specific hazards. The responsibility and accountability for occupational health and safety rested primarily with the employer who had to establish systems to identify existing and new hazards and regularly assess each hazard to determine whether or not it is significant. Other key aspects of the Act were training and supervision of workers as well as ensuring that workers were kept informed of all hazards they may encounter while at work. Monitoring of workers' health was also to be carried out if there is a possibility that hazards may cause immediate or long-term harm to their health. It also required the employer to keep a register of all accidents that occur and to notify the regulatory authority of any serious accident. Penalties for breaches under the HASIE Act were considerably more severe than was the case under the previous legislation, i.e. the Factories and Commercial Premises Act. A maximum fine of $100,000 or imprisonment for a maximum of one year, or both, were enforceable.

Yet despite the vast increases in penalties for non-compliance and publicity about high-profile court cases, the rate of workplace injuries, illness and fatalities failed to decline. Between June 1994 and June 2000 there were, on average, two work-related fatalities per week in New Zealand (New Zealand Department of Labour, 2000). Failure to significantly reduce the level of injuries, illness and fatalities was blamed by some on the fact that the HASIE Act 1992 deviated from the Robens' model of one authority administering one Act covering all workers and including joint participation in all health and safety matters. Specifically, the New Zealand HASIE Act did not incorporate formalised, joint participation mechanisms nor did it cover all workers.

As a result of these failures, the Labour-Alliance Coalition Government introduced the Health and Safety in Employment Amendment Act 2002 designed to address the gaps in the HASIE Act 1992 that were seen to impede its effectiveness. In parallel to the policy approach behind the original HASIE Act 1992, the Amendment Act 2002 was seen as complementing the Government's legislative initiatives in employment relations and accident compensation (Pashorina-Nichols, Lamm & Anderson, 2017). The common thread throughout the strategy for reform of the Act was the notion of partnership: joint employer, management, trade union and employee responsibility for improving health and safety performance. The substantive changes in the Amendment Act 2002 fell into five broad areas:

- *more comprehensive coverage* — the maritime, air and rail industries were included, coverage of mobile workers was confirmed, and protection was extended to some volunteers, persons receiving on the job training or work experience and "loaned employees". Court decisions establishing that the concept of "harm" under the HSIE Act covered work-related stress, and that a person's behaviour could be a "hazard" under the Act, were confirmed;
- *employee participation* — provision was made for good faith, co-operation ensuring employee participation in the decisions affecting health and safety, including mandatory elected health and safety representatives and health and safety committees in organisations with 30 or more employees;
- *enforcement* — more effective enforcement measures, including the imposition of infringement fees and hazard notices, were introduced;
- *penalties* — penalties for offences were increased significantly; and
- *indemnities* — indemnification against the costs of fines and infringement fees was prohibited.

These measures were also intended to comply with the International Labour Organisation's (ILO) conventions on health and safety, with particular reference to Convention 155 which requires governments to adopt coherent national OHS policy and law with the purpose of improving OHS in the workplace (see ILO Convention No. 155 Occupational Safety and Health Convention (adopted 22 June 1981); (Anderson, Hughes & Duncan 2017).

Health and Safety at Work Act 2015

As with previous occupational health and safety statutes, neither the HASIE Act 1992 nor the 2002 Amendment, stemmed the rise in workplace fatalities, injuries and illnesses in New Zealand. The 2010 Pike River Coal Mine explosion that killed 29 workers, the horrendous fatality rate in some sectors, such as forestry, and the 2010 and 2011 earthquakes that struck the Canterbury region killing over 180 people, resulted in a number of major safety reviews, notably the Royal Commission on the Pike River Coal Mine Tragedy 2012, the Royal Commission on the Canterbury Earthquakes 2012, the Independent Taskforce on Workplace Health and Safety 2013 and the Independent Forestry Safety Review 2014.

The recommendations outlined in the reports were remarkably similar in that there needed to be a stand-alone, well-resourced health and safety enforcement agency administrating legislation that reflected the current work practices and complex workplaces. A leadership and culture change at the senior management level was also recommended and that New Zealanders in general needed a much lower tolerance of risky, unsafe and unhealthy work. Finally, tripartism should operate at all levels. That is, the Government and employer and worker representative bodies should provide joint oversight of the system. Moreover, at an operational level, workers and employers need to actively engage with the regulator in developing regulations, codes of practice and guidance materials. In the workplace, workers should participate in the management of health and safety.

Introduced by the National Coalition Government in 2014, the occupational health and safety reform package was aimed at reducing New Zealand's workplace injury and death toll by 25% within a five-year period. The reforms saw the creation of a new and better resourced occupational health and safety enforcement agency, WorkSafe New Zealand, with occupational health and safety policy residing in the Ministry of Business, Innovation, and Employment. Although the new legislative framework continues the principles-based approach, it is heavily influenced by Australian legislation, the Work Health and Safety Act 2012. The new law, the Health and Safety at Work Act 2015 (HSWA), is supported by guidelines and introduced a number of key changes:

- A fundamental change to the definition of who is responsible for workplace health and safety. "Duty holder" will be replaced with the more inclusive concept of "a person conducting a business or undertaking" (PCBU). The term PCBU is intentionally broad in order to capture the broad range of working practices within New Zealand. In many cases, there will be several PCBUs working at the same workplace. For example, in a construction, there can be a principal contractor, contractor and sub-contractor all working on the same site. All parties are PCBUs under the new Act and as such are expected to manage the health and safety of those below them in the chain.
- Directors and other officers now have a duty to exercise due diligence to ensure that the organisation complies with health and safety duties and obligation.
- A shift from the "all practicable steps" test in the current legislation to a "reasonably practicable" test. The cost associated with available ways of eliminating or minimising risks will now be relevant to the assessment of what is reasonably practicable primarily when 'the cost is grossly disproportionate to the risk'.
- Under the new statute, there is not only a requirement to identify hazards but there is also more emphasis on managing current and potential risks. This means taking into consideration the potential for work-related health conditions as well as the injuries that could occur.
- All PCBUs must have worker engagement and participation practices, regardless of their size, level of risk or the type of work they carry out. That is, PCBUs must engage with workers on health and safety matters that will – or are likely to – affect them and provide reasonable opportunities for workers to participate effectively in improving health and safety on an ongoing basis.
- The roles of mandatory elected health and safety representatives

and health and safety committees were continued but the threshold was reduced to organisations with 20 or more employees.

Overall, the recent health and safety reforms that started in 2013 with the establishment of WorkSafe are certainly a move consistent with the Robens' model (Pashorina-Nichols et al., 2017). And while the number of work-related injuries, illnesses and fatalities have not reduced dramatically, the rates have stabilised. An independent inquiry, An Independent Report: Investigation and Prosecution – Reflective Learning Assessment, was undertaken as a result of a growing number of work-related injury and fatalities cases that WorkSafe either failed or did not complete an investigation/prosecution (Jones, 2019). The report concluded that there were major failings around: demand, workload and caseloads; investigation and investigator management; case management business model; victim focus; alignment and national consistency (Jones, 2019). Furthermore, there are still persistent and widespread issues, such as under-reporting of dangerous health and safety incidences, the lack of a basic understanding of how to manage risks in the workplace, etc. It is clear, therefore, that the health and safety of employees is still a work in progress.

Privacy Act

Background

Concerns over individual rights in respect of how personal information is collected, stored and accessed have been raised by New Zealanders over the years. By the 1990s, information was part of the New Zealand infrastructure brought about by the increased sophistication of information technology and new innovations in surveillance equipment. As a result, issues surrounding New Zealanders' privacy came to the fore and there was an urgent need to create legislation and an administrative structure that would advise on privacy issues and enforce the principles and policies under such legislation. There was also a need to develop contemporary guidelines that would be relevant to the workplace and that would complement other legislation, such as the Official Information Act 1982.

In 1991, the National Government enacted the Privacy Commissioner Act which established an administrative office and appointed a Commissioner before the Privacy Bill was passed. As a result, the Commissioner and staff were able to consult widely on privacy issues and investigate international trends in privacy law with the purpose of drafting legislation that would bring New Zealand's law in line with that of other countries and would reflect the growing global emphasis on individual rights (Longworth & McBride, 1994). The subsequent Privacy Act 1993 was hailed by the government as ground-breaking.

The Privacy Act 1993

The basic philosophy underlying the Privacy Act is that of individual autonomy: the individual has a right to know what personal information is held about him or her by an organisation and for what purpose this information will be used. Respecting this right requires openness and accountability. Furthermore, the Act has implemented this philosophy *by using principles rather than rules*. There are *12 basic principles* to which organisations must adhere, as listed below.

1. Personal information cannot be collected by an organisation unless it is done for a lawful purpose connected with a function or activity of the organisation and the collection of the information is necessary for that purpose.
2. Personal information can only be collected from the person concerned, unless the person agrees otherwise or the information is already public.
3. When personal information is collected from an individual, the organisation must ensure that the person is aware: of the purpose

of the collection; of who will hold the information, and of the individual's rights in respect of the information.

4. An organisation must ensure that personal information is not collected by unlawful means, or by means that are unfair or constitute an unreasonable intrusion on the personal affairs of the individual.
5. An organisation must also ensure that personal information is protected – using reasonable safeguards – against loss, unauthorised access and other misuse.
6. The organisation cannot keep personal information for longer than it is required for a lawful purpose.
7. A person is entitled to have access to the information held about him/her.
8. Requests made by an individual to have personal information corrected must be granted by the organisation concerned.
9. The organisation must ensure that personal information is accurate and not misleading.
10. Information collected for one purpose cannot be used for another.
11. An organisation cannot give information to anyone else unless that was part of the reason for its collection.
12. An organisation must not use personal identification numbers unless this is absolutely essential.

In summary, *the privacy principles concern the collection, storage, use and disclosure of personal information by any agency concerning an individual.* In the area of employment, these privacy principles are particularly relevant when: recruiting staff; terminating employment; managing staff; undertaking surveillance, drug-testing and medical screening. It, together with the Protected Disclosures Act 2020, also protects people who "blow the whistle" and disclosure of information in order to stop a particular unethical or illegal activity (see the Pugmire case, McGee, 2017). Under s 23 of the Act, every organisation is required to appoint a privacy officer to implement the legislation and monitor the organisation's activities with regard to privacy issues. Breaches of the legislation are dealt with by the Privacy Commissioner and staff who have the mandate to investigate complaints, provide conciliation and ultimately forward unresolved disputes to the Complaints Review Tribunal which, in turn, has the power to award compensatory remedies of up to $200 000.

Recent Reforms

There have been significant developments in information technology since the Privacy Act was introduced in 1993. More personal information than ever before has been collected, stored and disclosed using social media, e-commerce, internet-connected devices, cloud storage and other new technologies. Personal information can be easily distributed around the world and large quantities of data are readily stored, retrieved and disclosed. Privacy breaches are also occurring regularly and often on a global scale.

It was clear, therefore, that the Privacy Act 1993, needed to be updated. The New Zealand Law Commission's review of the Privacy Act in 2011 is the latest in a series of reviews. The Law Commissioners noted that the review of the Privacy Act was timely and called for the Privacy Act 1993 to be repealed and replaced with a modernised law. They also stated that:

> The Act is now 18 years old. In this modern age, technology, and its ability to gather, store and disseminate information about people, has advanced beyond anything imaginable in 1993. Much personal information is held by large agencies in both the public and private sectors. It can be sent to agencies overseas. It is very important to people that their personal information is properly protected, and that the law is flexible enough to be able to move with the times and provide that protection. (New Zealand Law Commission, 2011, p. IV)

However, the Privacy Commissioner at the time, John Edwards, argued that the Bill did not go far enough (see Privacy Commissioner Annual

Report, 2018a, p. 3). The Commissioner maintained that there was a need to be cognisant of the advances in technology as well as introducing meaningful consequences for non-compliance, that align with international best practice in a way that suits New Zealand's unique society. Notwithstanding Mr Edward's concerns, a new Privacy Act took effect from 1st December 2020, replacing the Privacy Act 1993. The 2020 Act supports early identification of systemic privacy risks and gives the Privacy Commissioner a stronger role. The changes also align New Zealand's privacy law with international developments, such as the 2013 OECD Privacy Guidelines and the European Union's General Data Protection Regulation. The Act incorporates key changes into New Zealand's privacy framework, such as mandating reporting of data breaches, strengthening cross-border data flow protections, and empowering the Commissioner to issue compliance notices and access directions. The key changes are listed below:

- *Requirements to report privacy breaches*: If an organisation has a privacy breach that causes serious harm or is likely to do so, it must notify the people affected and the Commissioner.
- *Compliance notices*: The Commissioner will be able to issue compliance notices to require an organisation to do something, or stop doing something.
- *Decisions on access requests*: The Commissioner will make binding decisions on complaints about access to information, rather than the Human Rights Review Tribunal. The Commissioner's decisions can be appealed to the Tribunal.
- *Strengthening cross-border protections*: New Zealand agencies will have to take reasonable steps to ensure that personal information sent overseas is protected by comparable privacy standards. The Act also clarifies that when a New Zealand organisation engages an overseas service provider, it will have to comply with New Zealand privacy laws.
- *Class actions*: The Act permits class actions in the Human Rights Review Tribunal by persons other than the Director of Human Rights Proceedings.

- *New criminal offences*: It will be an offence to mislead an organisation in a way that affects someone else's information, and to destroy documents containing personal information if a request has been made for it. The penalty will be a fine of up to $10,000.
- *Strengthening the Privacy Commissioner's information gathering power*: The Commissioner will be able to shorten the timeframe in which an organisation must comply with investigations and the penalty for non-compliance will be increased from $2,000 to 10,000.

Privacy Issues

One of the major concerns regarding privacy in New Zealand and elsewhere is the *misuse and appropriation of personal information*. A 2018 survey commissioned by the Privacy Commissioner (2018b) showed that over half the people surveyed (67 percent) were concerned about their individual privacy. Respondents felt particularly vulnerable when sharing personal information over social media, for example, when posting personal information on one's career. Sixty-five percent of those surveyed were uncomfortable about submitting information on the web and 75% had little or no confidence at all that their electronic information would be secure. The 2018 survey also showed that New Zealanders were most concerned about organisations sharing personal information with other organisations (79%). While sixty-two percent of New Zealanders said they trusted government organisations with their personal information, trust in private sector organisations was significantly lower at 32 percent.

The other area of contention is how the Privacy Act 1993 principles conflict with the practice of *drug testing and employee surveillance*. Increasingly, employers are implementing surveillance and drug-testing regimes as health and safety measures in order to offset the likelihood that they will be prosecuted if a worker is injured while under the influence of drugs or alcohol, or observed to have committed a hazardous act. However, unions state that drug testing and surveillance contravene the principles and the tenets of the Privacy Act. Unions and workers argue that, on the one hand, employers are invoking the principles of the Privacy Act and are reluctant to divulge information pertinent to workers' health and safety, yet on the other hand, they are ignoring the Privacy Act when implementing drug-testing and employee-surveillance schemes to mitigate health-and-safety fines. In a detailed analysis of the issues surrounding the Privacy Act, McIntosh (1995, p. 50) states:

> Conformity to the Privacy Act principles is an essential part of a drug testing program. A term in a contract which permits drug testing will therefore need to ensure that the employees to be tested have full information about the testing procedures, and the nature of the information which will be passed to the employer by the drug testing laboratory. Employers will provide employees with this full information if they ensure that the term conforms to the Privacy Act principles.

The Office of the Privacy Commission (2018) also advises that an employer may only require employees and other workers to submit to alcohol or drugs tests if this is a condition of their appointment and recorded in the employment agreement or other document. Employees should follow all legal and reasonable requests from their employer. Whether or not it is reasonable for an employer to require an employee to undertake a drug test depends on a variety of different factors. It can mean balancing two factors, for example, drug testing may be necessary to protect the safety of employees but may also be viewed as an unreasonable intrusion into the privacy of employees. Testing for alcohol or drugs is much more difficult if it is not in the employment agreement. In short, employers thinking about drug testing employees should seek legal advice.

The increasing use by organisations of *surveillance* of their employees and customers is also controversial. Current technology enables employers to spy on their employees by tapping telephones, reading e-mail messages and monitoring computer screens. They can bug conversations, analyse computer and keyboard work, peer through close-circuit television cameras to monitor personal movements and analyse urine to detect drug use (illicit or otherwise). In a judgment concerning the surveillance of an employee, the Privacy Commissioner commented that under Principle 3 (see p. 89), the employer must make all reasonable efforts to ensure the person knows that information is being collected, what it will be used for, to whom it will be passed on, and the consequences of not providing the information (Slane, 1995). However, he added that under certain circumstances there are reasonable grounds to conduct surveillance without the consent of the employee. These circumstances are as follows:

- it is not reasonably practicable to draw the fact of surveillance to the employee's attention if the surveillance is intended to reveal covert and unlawful behaviour (Information Privacy Principles (IPP) 3(4)(e));
- it would prejudice the purpose of collection of information if the employee is told that he/she is under surveillance;
- non-compliance with Principle 3 is necessary to gain sufficient evidence of theft to enable prosecution of an offender before a court (IPP 3(4)c(iv)).

More recently, it was revealed that a large number of government agencies were using a private security firm to carry out the surveillance of members of the public. Instigated by the Public Service Commission (2018), the subsequent inquiry into the use of external security consultants by government agencies, found that multiple government agencies not only broke the public service code of conduct in their use of private investigators to spy on an array of people including earthquake claimants and protesters, but also contravened the principles of the Privacy Act. It was also noted in the report that the law in this area is complex and developing. However, it is clear that surveillance by government agencies without a warrant may be unlawful if it involves an unlawful invasion of privacy; that is, a surveillance activity will amount to the tort of invasion of privacy if it is a highly offensive and unauthorised intrusion into seclusion in breach of a reasonable expectation of privacy (Martin & Mount, 2018, p. 21).

Thus, new technology continues to pose a challenge when it comes to ensuring that individuals' privacy rights are upheld in the workplace. As more judgments are made by the Complaints Review Tribunal and the courts in terms of the Privacy Act, 2020 controversial or 'grey' areas, such as surveillance, drug testing and withholding or disclosing information, will become clearer. However, as happens with the Human Rights legislation, breaches of the Privacy Act continue to occur, with a number of public sector organisations repeatedly being listed as receiving more complaints than other organisations (Privacy Commissioner's Annual Report, 2021). This point is particularly interesting, since the public sector is frequently seen as leading the way in advancing human rights and equal employment opportunities (EEO).

Human Rights Act

Human rights – an overview

Early examples of human rights-type legislation can be found in protective employment laws, such as the Females' Act 1873, the Employment of Females and Others Act 1881, the Factories Act of 1894 and the Industrial Conciliation and Arbitration Act 1894. These Acts contained pro-human rights sentiments in that they set minimum standards of wages and conditions and allowed freedom of association (e.g. membership of trade unions). Also, New Zealand has been a signatory to the United Nations and International Labour Organisation (ILO) declarations and covenants on human rights since 1948.

However, traditionally law and policies on human rights lacked clarity and were contradictory and selective. The absence of anti-discriminatory laws fostered prejudice in New Zealand employment for over a century by favouring the rights of European men at the expense of women, children, physically and mentally impaired people and non-European workers. Furthermore, the practice of ensuring that men's wages were higher than women's and the segregation of women into a handful of occupations impeded the process of ensuring equality of the sexes in the workforce.

Throughout the 1960s and 1970s there was growing public disquiet about the continuing discriminatory practices in the workplace and in the wider society. One of the first pieces of human rights legislation was passed in 1960 and it promoted employment opportunities for people with disabilities. However, the movement to enforce equal pay and equal employment opportunities by law and to address the principles of the Treaty of Waitangi was led primarily by those working in the public sector. As a result, human rights principles became embedded in key public service employment legislation such as the Government Services Equal Pay Act 1960, the State-Owned Enterprises Act 1986 and the State Sector Act 1988.

The 1970s and 1980s saw the introduction of a succession of human rights legislation, aimed at curbing discriminatory practices in the workplace. The first such piece of legislation was the Race Relations Act 1971, and six years later the Human Rights Commission Act 1977 established the Human Rights Commission and the Equal Opportunities Tribunal. The Human Rights Commission Act prohibited discrimination on the grounds of: sex; race; colour; ethnic or national origin; marital status, and religious or ethical beliefs for employment, public access, provision of goods and services, accommodation and education. Sexual harassment was defined as discrimination under this Act. Twelve years after the passing of the Government Services Equal Pay Act, the Equal Pay Act 1972 was finally passed and applied to all private-sector workers.

During its 1984–1990 term, the Labour Government established the Ministry of Women's Affairs (now known as the Ministry for Women), and then enacted the Employment Equity Act 1990 which went further than any other legislation to address employment inequities. When it was elected in 1990, one of the first actions of the National Government was to repeal the Employment Equity Act in 1990, but it enacted the Human Rights Act 1993 which replaced the Race Relations Act and the Human Rights Commission Act. While the Human Rights Act used the unlawful discrimination categories from the Human Rights Commission Act 1977, it was more wide-ranging and included categories such as age, disability, political opinion, employment status, family status and sexual orientation.

Complaints involving discrimination on the grounds of race, colour, national or ethnic origin covered under the Human Rights Act are currently dealt with by the Race Relations Office. The Office of the Race Relations Conciliator was first established by the Race Relations Act 1971 and currently has the responsibility of administering those parts of the Act that pertain to racial discrimination or racial harassment under the Human Rights Act 1993. For reasons of bureaucratic efficiency, the Office of the Race Relations Conciliator was consolidated with the Human Rights Commission by an amendment to the Human Rights Act in 2001. There are four Human Rights Commissioners – one of which is the Race Relations Commissioner.

The Human Rights Act 1993

The Human Rights Act protects both those seeking employment and those in employment and there is a wide variety of grounds on which it is unlawful to discriminate. The Human Rights Commission (1997, p. 1) states that:

> Discrimination occurs where, under the same circumstances, someone is treated less favourably than someone else. Discrimination also exists where a condition is imposed which, although the same for everyone, unfairly disadvantages some people.

According to the Act, where a job applicant or an employee is qualified for particular job, it is unlawful for an employer or an employment agency to discriminate on the grounds listed below.

- Sex, which includes pregnancy and childbirth and sexual orientation, meaning a heterosexual, homosexual, lesbian or bisexual orientation.
- Marital status, which includes being single, married, separated, divorced, widowed or in a de facto relationship.
- Family status, which includes having or not having responsibility for children or other dependants; being married to or being a relative of a particular person.
- Religious, ethical beliefs or political opinion, including not having a political opinion.
- Ethnic or national origins, which includes nationality and citizenship.
- Disability, which includes physical or psychiatric illness, and most disabilities, including presence in the body of organisms capable of causing disease.
- Age, which provides protection from the age of 16. There is no upper age limit on discrimination.
- Employment status; that is, being unemployed or a beneficiary.

There are, however, exceptions that occur where discrimination is applied for genuine reasons as a qualification for a job. An example is requiring bar staff to be over 18 years of age in order to serve in licensed premises.

The primary function of the Human Rights Commission is to deal with complaints under the Human Rights Act, 1993, which its officers will have to investigate. Its officers might then have to conciliate with the aim of achieving a settlement. The key concepts driving the settlement process are that the complainant has suffered discrimination and that a remedy is necessary to put the matter right. Where possible, the Commission will make all efforts to conciliate a settlement in a way that is agreeable to both parties. The benefits of choosing the conciliation option are that it is usually quicker than an investigation, it involves fewer people, and it often assists the parties involved in restoring and maintaining a better working relationship. However, in most cases an officer will be required to investigate the substance of the complaint while at the same time endeavouring to reach a settlement. Settlements may include any of the following:

- apologies
- assurance that the behaviour complained of will not be repeated
- money to compensate for hurt feelings, loss of wages, counselling, and so on
- access to services previously denied
- equal employment opportunity or sexual harassment prevention programmes, counselling or education.

If a settlement cannot be reached, then the Director of Human Rights Proceedings will make the decision on an application for legal representation in the Human Rights Review Tribunal. The Complaints Review Tribunal hears complaints not only from the Human Rights Commission, but also from the Race Relations Conciliator, Privacy Commissioner and Health and Disability Commissioner. Like a judicial court, the Complaints Review Tribunal involves the process of litigation and has the power not only to award compensation to the Proceeding Commissioner on behalf of the complainant but also to make various orders, such as requiring the respondent to apologise to the complainant.

Discrimination issues

The number of complaints has increased substantially over the years. In 2017 there were 1392 enquiries and complaints alleging unlawful discrimination over the year, 1274 of which were classified as unlawful discrimination complaints – a 14% increase of complaints received the previous year. However, by 2020 there was an exponential increase in the number of complaints and enquiries, in which the Human Rights Commission received 5915 new enquiries and complaints, and of those, 1445 were complaints of alleged unlawful discrimination. Of the 1445 complaints of alleged unlawful discrimination the Human Rights Commission (2021a) received in 2019-20, the five main grounds cited were: 1) 'race-related' complaints (383); 2) disability (249); 3) sex (110); 4) age (93); and, 5) sexual harassment (69). These five grounds have been consistently the most cited over recent years.

As part of their core business, the Human Rights Commission has produced numerous reviews and submissions (see https://www.hrc.co.nz/resources/). More recently, the Commission has, for example, compiled submissions to: the Productivity Commission's on immigration (2021); the Petitions Committee supporting the prohibition of modern slavery (2021); and the Ministry of Justice on restricting the incitement of hatred and discrimination (2021). In their submission to the Productivity Commission, the Human Rights Commission stated that it is important to apply a human rights lens to the issue of immigration, that respect for human rights should be at the heart of any immigration policy review, and that flexibility must be embraced in the way that the immigration operations are conducted.

Moreover, in response to a growing number of cases of modern slavery, in which most of the cases involved the exploited migrant workers, the Human Rights Commission has supported the need to enact anti-slavery legislation similar to the legislation in the UK and Australia. Protecting workers' rights is also evident in the Human Rights Commission's submission to the Ministry of Justice on preventing incitement of hatred and discrimination. Here they argued that it is important that offensive, insulting, abusive comments targeted at particular groups are called out as being unacceptable in the diverse, inclusive society of contemporary New Zealand.

Many of the complaints concerned discrimination on the grounds of disability. Currently, about 1 in 5 or 1.1 million New Zealanders has a disability (Disability Commission, 2021). In the Human Rights Act, disability covers the following:

- physical disability or impairment (e.g. respiratory conditions)
- physical illness
- psychiatric illness (e.g. depression or schizophrenia)
- intellectual or psychological disability or impairment (e.g. learning disorders)
- any other loss or abnormality of psychological, physiological or anatomical structure or function (e.g. arthritis or amputation)
- reliance on a guide dog, wheelchair or other remedial means the presence in the body of organisms capable of causing illness (e.g. HIV/AIDS or hepatitis).

In an effort to address the complex issues around disability, the Labour Coalition Government established the Office for Disability Issues in 2002 to assist the Minister for Disability Issues (see https://www.odi.govt.nz/). Sitting within the Ministry of Social Development, the Office for Disability Issues promotes action and monitors implementation and progress to improve the lives of those who have a disability. The Office also supports the implementation of the United Nations Convention on the Rights of Persons with Disabilities and the New Zealand Disability Strategy.

In a recent speech, the Disability Rights Commissioner, Paula Tesoriero noted that while advances had been made in the area of disability, there were still outstanding issues. For example, 43% of young disabled New Zealanders aged between 15-24 years are not in education, employment or training compared with 10% of non-disabled people. She also noted that only 25% of disabled people participate in the workforce, compared with 75% of non-disabled people and that the unemployment rate of disabled people is more than double the rate of non-disabled (Disabilities Commission, 2019).

In a study on the working experiences of people with disabilities, van Dalen (2017) also notes that people who are living with a disability are vastly overrepresented in New Zealand's poverty figures, and 74% of those who are not in work want to be working. His study indicates that there is an increased likelihood of people with disabilities having lower incomes than people without disabilities. This is largely due to the high living costs and low incomes of people with disabilities. However, Disability Commission, (2021) argues that employing people with disabilities is beneficial to employers. Generally, such workers are loyal and committed employees, rate higher on attendance, and are less likely to take sick leave. Employees with disabilities improve wider organisational performance, increase understanding of customers with disabilities, and can raise standards and expectations of all employees. According to the Disability Commission, (2021), many of the costs involved in employing people with disabilities are one-off and often smaller than expected.

While complaints on the grounds of disability represent a significant portion of overall complaints received by Human Rights Commission, the Commission also received a large number of complaints on the basis of race, colour, national or ethnic origin. Since the outbreak of COVID-19 in 2020, the Human Rights Commission noted that there had been a parallel rise in the number of complaints of discrimination and racism by people from the Chinese, Asian, Māori and Pacific Island communities. The results from a survey led by the Human Rights Commission also showed that more than half of Māori and Chinese respondents experienced some form of discrimination, and Chinese had much greater concerns about their personal safety compared with other respondents. The most common forms of racism and discrimination reported by the nearly 2000 respondents were online and face-to-face negative racist and xenophobic comments, abuse, threats of violence and spitting. Māori and those of the Asian and Chinese community stated that their experiences of discrimination and racial abuse meant they struggled to feel a sense of belonging and they suffered mentally and emotionally because of it (Human Rights Commission, 2021b).

Discrimination on the basis of age and sex are also perennial issues. In a 2018 survey by the Commission for Financial Capability (now Te Ara Ahunga Ora Retirement Commission), over half of respondents felt that when applying for a job they were discriminated against on the basis of age (Commission for Financial Capability 2018). Moreover, while age and sex discrimination occur in a broad spectrum of occupations, they are more noticeable in the professional and managerial occupations. For example, in 2020 women held only 22.5% of board director roles and 25.4% of senior leadership positions in New Zealand Stock Exchange (NZX) listed companies (Ministry for Women, 2021). In addition, women made up 53.2% of the top three tiers of the public service, and half of its chief executives in 2020. While there is currently no official statistics on private sector pay gaps by industry or occupation, the Ministry for Women has been collecting data on the public sector. The public service gender pay gap has fallen to 9.6% by 2020 – the lowest gap since measurements began 20 years ago (Ministry for Women, 2021).

The Human Rights Commission, and other government agencies, have also had to respond to the public revelations of sexual harassment in high profile organisations. The international #MeToo movement, which was intended to expose sexual harassment in the entertainment industry, together with heightened media reporting of sexual harassment, put the spotlight on the issue in New Zealand. Up until 2018 data on the extent of the problem was scant. In the absence of any research, the national media outlet Stuff used the Official Information Act to investigate the scale of sexual harassment across nearly 1400 public organisations, employing 273,000 people (Anthony, 2018).

The audit revealed that the number of sexual harassment complaints increased year on year. In 2015 there were just 70 complaints, in 2016 there were 88 and in 2017 it spiked to 139. In the first four months of 2018 there were 60 complaints – which is tracking towards 180 by year's end. The audit also highlighted major failings in how the organisations had responded to those complaints. One of the smallest organisations, Film Commission, with just 40 staff, had the highest rate of harassment: four female complainants in the past three years; three men accused of harassment. In all the cases, the commission treated the complaints as "informal" and resolved them "informally" (Anthony, 2018).

In response to the rise in the number of sexual harassment complaints, the Public Service Commission in 2019 initiated a system wide-work programme, led by two Public Sector chief executives. According to the Public Service Commission (2021), the work programme will help agencies to have work environments where people enjoy what they do, are respected for who they are, and contribute to the maximum of their potential.

Conclusion

Since 1992, occupational health and safety, privacy and human rights legislation has ensured that New Zealanders have some protection against the infringement of their rights. However, the onus is on the *individual* to seek redress for breaches of the legislation. The primary role of the occupational health and safety, privacy, human rights officers is investigative, relying almost entirely on incoming complaints. However, relying on the individual to make a complaint is problematic. There is growing evidence to show that there is a large degree of under-reporting of occupational health and safety, privacy and human rights violations against a backdrop of unemployment and insecure work. Recognising this perennial issue, the Race Relations Conciliator noted that:

> Because employment involves people's livelihoods and working environments, it is easy to understand why employees may be reluctant to complain. They may be fearful of their employer's response to a complaint and therefore choose not to take this course of action ... Employment-related discrimination, however, represents the primary area of complaint, despite our numbers placing it in third position. (Office of the Race Relations Conciliator, 2000, p. 29)

In spite of the many issues outlined in this chapter, there is no doubt that the three Acts have had a significant impact on employment relations. The substantial fines that can be imposed for breaches of the legislation have caused employers to rethink the way they manage their staff and the working environment they provide. In particular, there has been increased efforts between government agencies and employer and worker organisations to adopt a more collaborative approach in which there is a move away from the neo-liberal, market orientated approach to one that encourages employee involvement and is aligned more with the tenets of the Employment Relations Act of good fair bargaining and employee democracy.

References

Anderson, G., Hughes, J., and Duncan, D. (2017). (2nd ed). *Employment Law in New Zealand.* LexisNexis NZ Limited.

Anthony, J. (2018). 'Sexual harassment complaints double: Behind everyone is a human story'. Stuff, 2nd September, https://www.stuff.co.nz/business/industries/106471651/sexual-harassment-in-public-sector-nearly-doubles-since-2015

Campbell, I. B. (1992). From no fault to own fault? Changes in OSH regulations. *Journal of Occupational Health and Safety—Aust. & NZ, 8* (1), 3-4.

Commission for Financial Capability. (2018). *Ageing Workforce: Business- Survey Results.* Commission for Financial Capability New Zealand.

Disability Commission. (2021). *Annual Report.* Health & Disability Commission New Zealand.

Human Rights Commission. (2019). *Disability Rights in Aotearoa New Zealand – Where Have We Got To?* Paula Tesoriero, Disability Rights

Commissioner, https://www.hrc.co.nz/news/disability-rights-aotearoa-new-zealand-12-years-where-have-we-got/

Human Rights Commission. (2022). Annual Report 2019-2020. https://www.hrc.co.nz/news/latest-annual report-released/

Human Rights Commission. (2021). Prevalence and Patterns of Racism and Xenophobia in the Covid-19 Context: A focus on Chinese and Asian communities, https://apo.org.au/node/311028

Human Rights Commission. (2020). Annual Report. https://www.hrc.co.nz/files/8116/0850/9706/ HRC_Annual_Report_19-20_FINAL.pdf.

Human Rights Commission. (1997). Pre-Employment Guidelines: Based on the Human Rights Act 1993. Auckland: Human Rights Commission.

Jones, G. (2019). *An Independent Report: Investigation and Prosecution – Reflective Learning Assessment*, WorkSafe New Zealand.

Lamm, F., Rasmussen, E. and Anderson, A. (2013). The Case of the Disappearing Department of Labour: Whither goes state protection for vulnerable workers. In Sargeant, M. and Ori, M. (Eds.). *Vulnerable Workers and Precarious Work* (pp. 184-219). Cambridge Scholars Publishing.

Longworth, E., and McBride, T. (1994). *The Privacy Act: A guide.* GP Publications.

McIntosh, I. (1995). Employee Drug Testing in New Zealand. LLB Thesis, University of Auckland.

McGee, D. (2017). Ombudsmen and Officers of Parliament: Ombudsmen – whistleblowing. *Te Ara, The Encyclopaedia of New Zealand.* https://teara.govt.nz/en/ombudsmen-and-officers-of-parliament/page-5

Martin, D. and Mount, S. QC. (2018). 'Inquiry into the use of external security consultants by Government Agencies'. Public Service Commission.

Ministry for Women. (2021). Annual Report of Manatū Wāhine Ministry for Women. https://women.govt.nz/documents/annual-report-2021

New Zealand Department of Labour. (2000). The Costs and Benefits of Complying with the HSE Act 1992. The Department of Labour Occasional Paper Series 2001/4. Wellington: DOL with the Ministry of Economic Development.

New Zealand Law Commission. (2011). 'Review of the Privacy Act 1993: Review of the Law of Privacy Stage 4'. [2011] NZLCR 123.

Office of the Race Relations Conciliator. (2000). Annual Report. Human Rights Commission.

Pashorina-Nichols, V., Lamm, F. and Anderson, G. (2017). Reforming workplace health and safety regulation: Second time lucky. In Anderson, G., Geare, A., Rasmussen, E. & Wilson, M. (Eds.). *Transforming workplace relations in New Zealand 1976-2016* (pp. 129-148). Victoria University Press.

Privacy Commissioner. (2018a). *Annual Report of the Privacy Commissioner.* Privacy Commission New Zealand.

Privacy Commissioner. (2018b). *Privacy Concerns and Sharing Data.* Privacy Commission New Zealand.

Public Sector Commission (2021). Positive and Safe Workplaces. https://www.publicservice.govt.nz/resources/positive-and-safe-workplaces/

Robens, L. (1972). Report of the Committee on Safety and Health at Work. *London: Majesty's Stationery Office.*

Slane, B. (1995). Privacy Commissioner's Case Notes. Case Note: 0632. Privacy Commissioner, January.

van Dalen, D. (2017). *Acknowledging ability: Overcoming the barriers to employment for people living with disabilities*. Maxim Institute., https://www.maxim.org.nz/article/acknowledging-ability/

Current Legislation

Accident Compensation Act 2001

Employment Relations Act 2000

Equal Pay Act 1972

Health and Safety at Work Act 2015

Human Rights Act 1993

Official Information Act 1982

Privacy Act 2020

Privacy Commissioner Act 1991

Public Service Act 2020

Race Relations Act 1971

State Owned Enterprises Act 1986

State Sector Act 1988

International Instruments

European Union General Data Protection Regulation (EU 2016/679)

International Labour Organisation Occupational Safety and Health Convention, 1981 (No. 155)

OECD Guidelines Governing the Protection of Privacy and Transborder Flows of Personal Data (Adopted 23 September 1980, Amended 11 July 2013, Follow-up report 2021)

United Nations Universal Declaration of Human Rights 1948

Enquiries

Independent Forestry Safety Review 2014

Independent Taskforce on Workplace Health and Safety 2013

Royal Commission on the Canterbury Earthquakes 2012

Royal Commission on the Pike River Coal Mine Tragedy 2012

6. Changing work, employment and workplace practices

ERLING RASMUSSEN; GEMMA PIERCY-CAMERON; AND MICHAEL FLETCHER

1. To overview labour market changes and several embedded labour market and employment relations problems
2. To identify how the Covid-19 pandemic has influenced labour market and employment relations trends
3. To consider the main changes in vocational education and training
4. To outline the main reasons for perennial low productivity growth and how this can be reversed in the future
5. To present changes in employee participation and the limited role of mandatory participation structures

Introduction

New Zealand employment relations have experienced considerable changes over the last decades as shown in chapters 3, 4 and 5. This chapter deals with some of these changes and the associated trends and issues. It starts with an overview of labour market changes which highlights both stability and radical changes. Many of these changes were facilitated originally by the ECA 1991 and, since then, are linked to concerns about casualisation, low wages, gender and ethnicity issues, long working hours and 'underemployment'. Similar concerns are also expressed in the 'future of work' debate though a sharp rise in casualisation, self-employment and short working hours is yet to occur.

While many economic and employment relations reforms were often premised on future gains the so-called neo-liberal 'New Zealand Experiment' never delivered the high wage, high skill, highly productive economy. Despite some public policy changes in the new millennium, there are still a prevalence of low wages, skill shortages and low productivity growth. There have been much research and many reports but there are still embedded labour market issues and a concerning lack of employment relations consensus regarding broadly based solutions. Will New Zealand continue to be reliant on importing overseas workers during economic upswings, sliding in international measures of productivity levels and living standards, and having weak information and consultation standards for employees?

The advent of the Covid-19 pandemic in 2020 prompted major short-term policy responses and may present new perspectives on the development of the New Zealand economy and labour market. The move towards a post-industrial society (Bell, 1974) was much slower in New Zealand until the opening of market access following the 'New Zealand Experiment' from 1984 onwards. However, even now primary industries are very important and being a producer of various form of food is properly regarded more positively following the Covid-19 pandemic. Although it is now seen as problematic that the decline of manufacturing and resultant reliance on overseas goods has created a certain level of vulnerability as has the strong growth in international tourism and hospitality. At the time of writing, it is unclear how much the temporary economic and labour market upheavals due to the pandemic will result in lasting changes or what the long-term outcomes will be.

Labour market issues

As can be seen from Figure 6.1 the New Zealand labour market has experienced strong employment growth and relatively low unemployment for most of the new millennium. The exception has been the Global Financial Crisis years, although even in those years, the unemployment rate was considerably below the OECD average. The expansion of employment and a rise in participation rate have been very strong and the participation rate has been one of highest amongst the OECD countries in recent years. These increases have coincided with an unprecedented influx of permanent migrants and of workers on temporary visas. Normally, net migration figures would oscillate between plus or minus 20,000 but net migration reached over 60,000 per annum under the 2014-2017 National-led government. By December 2020, the working age population (that is the usually resident population aged 15 years or over) stood at 4,094,000. This number comprised 2,748,000 people in employment, 141,000 who were unemployed, and 1,205,000 people who were not participating in the labour force (based on Statistics NZ's Quarterly Series).

Figure 6.1 Labour force participation, employment and unemployment rates, 1986–2020

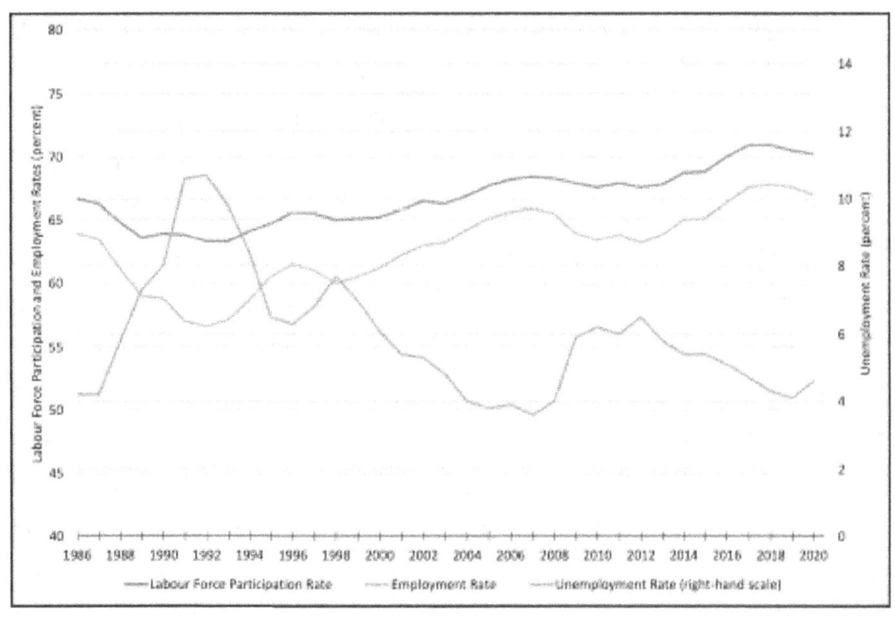

Source: Household Labour Force Survey, Statistic New Zealand

Covid-19 and the labour market

At time of writing in early 2022, New Zealand, like the rest of the world, is still influenced by the Covid-19 pandemic. New Zealand's public health response has been highly successful, with just over 100 deaths recorded in March 2022. This is one of the lowest death rates per capita in the world. New Zealand's economic and labour market response has also proven successful. The strategy of containing the virus domestically and maintaining strict border controls limited the impact on business activity, except in specific industries such as tourism and aviation. The Government's large-scale wage subsidy scheme, although costly at over $14 billion by September 2021, was also effective in tiding most workers and employers over periods where many firms were forced to close either because of the Government-imposed lockdowns or for lack of custom. Other smaller schemes also helped with business continuity.

The uncertainty created by the Covid-19 pandemic has prompted wild predictions and significant fluctuations in labour market statistics. Early estimates that the effects of the pandemic might result in the unemployment rate rising to 8% or even higher have proven incorrect. The unemployment rate jumped from 3.9% in the June quarter 2020 to 5.1% in the September quarter but has since fallen back to 3.2% in late 2021. Similarly, the total number of people in employment, which had fallen by 42,000 in the first half of 2020 has returned to pre-Covid levels, although industries such as tourism and accommodation remain well below pre-Covid levels. Female employment fell more than male employment in the March and June 2020 quarters (negative 23,400 compared to negative 19,100) fuelling talk of a 'shecession'; however, it also bounced back strongly. Still, a strong construction upswing and subdued hospitality and retail sectors have favoured male employment over female employment in 2021.

With the borders still mostly closed in 2021, sectors that have come to rely on temporary overseas labour, such as horticulture, tourism and hospitality, and some parts of agriculture, have been pressing government to allow more temporary workers to enter the country. To date, the Government's main response has been to extend the existing temporary visas and provide a pathway to residency of those temporary workers already in New Zealand. There has also been targeted, restricted entry of some overseas workers, for example as part of the Recognised Seasonal Employer (RSE) Scheme.

Labour market and employment trends

Employment demands have been influenced by a certain level of catch-up of infrastructure shortfalls in previous decades but the Global Financial Crisis, the Christchurch earthquakes and repairing 'leaky buildings' have added to demand pressures in construction. The accommodation of unusually high net migration between 2013 and 2020 has also put pressure on the domestic construction industry. Besides construction, several sectors have experienced skills shortages and employer organisations have advocated fewer restrictions on permanent and temporary migrant workers. In particular, the tourism and hospitality sector had experienced very strong growth and, at least up until the border closure in March 2020, it had become our biggest income earner. It is too early to tell how tourism and hospitality will evolve post-Covid, whether it will revert to something similar to the pre-Covid period or whether both the number and 'mix' of tourists and employees will be different in future?

Many other OECD countries would envy the employment, unemployment and participation record of New Zealand over the last couple of decades. However, there are number of seriously embedded labour issues which have yet to be solved (OECD, 2019). As discussed below, the fundamental problem of low productivity growth has persisted, and this has been associated with an on-going decline in *relative* living standards and wealth. Economic growth has mainly been achieved by higher labour utilisation where more people have worked more (longer working hours) and, since the early 1990s, with the creation a relatively low paid workforce. Traditionally, skills shortages have been a companion of economic upswings, and this has also been the situation in most years in the new millennium (see next section). Thus, skill shortages have often been a major employer concern and have restrained economic growth, but this has yet to lead to fundamental shifts in pay levels or widespread business investment in vocational training and productivity-enhancing processes.

With the internationalisation of the New Zealand economy and with a strong growth in service sector jobs, concerns have been raised about a move towards a more flexible labour market with fewer full-time and less secure jobs (Groot et al., 2017). Whether it is called vulnerable work, employment insecurity, casualisation or precarious work these terms indicate expectations of a labour market which has less predictability in incomes, employment, and career progression. As shown in chapters 3 and 4, the New Zealand labour market has moved away from a historical high level of employment security since the comprehensive policy reforms of the 1980s and 1990s. The 'future of work' debate has also created widespread concerns about the risk of a labour market dominated by the 'gig economy' and a decline in permanent full-time employment (NZ Productivity Commission, 2019; Stewart & Stanford, 2017). That said, at least up until the Covid-19 pandemic, trends in official New Zealand statistics of various atypical employment types appear to have stabilised following the post-2008 Global Financial Crisis (see below).

When employment insecurity is measured the most commonly used statistical indicators are full-time versus part-time jobs, employees versus self-employed, and the extent of temporary and casual employment. As discussed below, there are many part-time jobs and a considerable number of self-employed, but the level of part-time jobs and self-employment have been relatively stable as a proportion of the workforce. These trends indicate that economic upswings have tended to generate as many full-time jobs as other forms of work. There have only been official statistics on the extent of temporary and casual employment since the 2008 Survey of Working Life. As can be seen in Table 6.2, this survey has now run another three times since 2008 and temporary and casual employment has been stable and fluctuated around or below 10% of the total employed population. Thus, the fragmented labour market of the 'future of work' has yet to arrive, according to the official statistics trends.

In the last three decades, part-time employees have constituted around 20% of all employees (according to the Household Labour Force Survey by Statistics New Zealand). There were 20.1% in December 1990, 22.5% in December 2000, 22.1% in December 2010 and 19.8% in December 2020. While the proportion of part-time employment has been fairly stable at around one-fifth of all employees, as the workforce has grown so, too, has the number of part-timers. As the number of employees increased from 1,535,000 in December 1990 to 2,831,000 in December 2021, part-time employees have risen from 308,535 in 1990 to 567,000 in December 2021. It is still predominantly women who are working part-time and that probably have some negative consequences in terms of career progression (see below).

Table 6.2 distinguishes between self-employed and employers by only including self-employed with no employees. As with part-time employment, Table 6.2 illustrates a remarkable stability in the proportion of self-employed in respect of the total employed population. While there can be advantages in being self-employed (see Chapter 1), there are also risks and uncertainties in terms of income volatility and work fluctuation where self-employed can experience a 'famine or feast' situation with lots or very few offers of work. Additionally, there are some sectors – for example, construction – where many jobs are designed to be self-employment and that can leave limited choice for workers. Finally, it is important to note that a significant part of the total employed population – nearly 20% – consist of employers and self-employed.

Thus, while we emphasise *limited* fluctuation in the general types of employment there are still types of employment where work and employment fluctuations are a constant part of work experiences.

There are also many groups in the labour market with a tenuous relationship to job and career opportunities and these groups *may* grow proportionally in the coming years as indicated by the current debates about the 'future of work', the 'gig economy' and precarious work (see below).

Table 6.2 Paid employees, employers, and self-employed as percent of total employed population

	Employees	Employers	Self-employed, no employees
Dec 1990	80.2	7.8	10.5
Dec 1995	79.1	7.0	12.7
Dec. 2000	81.4	6.5	11.4
Dec. 2005	83.7	4.5	10.6
Dec. 2010	85.1	3.6	10.3
Dec. 2015	80.2	6.5	12.4
Dec. 2020	80.2	7.8	10.5

Source: Household Labour Force Survey, Statistic New Zealand

Note: totals do not sum to 100 because a small number of unpaid family workers has been excluded.

As shown in Table 6.3, there is so far no sign of a growth in temporary employment arrangements. Since the first official statistics in 2008, the total figures of temporary employment arrangements have been stable around 10% (with the 8.6% figure in 2020 probably being influenced by Covid-19 impacts). Likewise, the different forms of temporary employment relationships have also remained more or less stable over the same period. Generally, women are slightly more likely than men to be in temporary employment arrangements: 10.6% compared to 8.2%.

Compared to other OECD countries, New Zealand has an above average percentage of part-time employees, an about average proportion of self-employed and a slightly below average share of workers in temporary employment relationships. A key point, though, is that, across the OECD as a whole, there is no observable rise in casualised employment, at least as far as these very broad indicators are concerned. (Fletcher & Rasmussen, 2019: 36).

Table 6.3 The main categories of 'temporary' working arrangements as percent of total employed population (main job)

	Casual work	Fixed-term employment	Temping	Seasonal employment	TOTAL
2008 (Mar qtr)	4.0	1.9	0.6	3.2	9.6
2012 (Dec qtr)	4.1	2.6	0.7	3.5	10.9
2016 (Dec qtr)	5.2	2.8	0.5	1.4	9.9
2020 (Dec qtr)	4.9	2.3	0.4	1.0	8.6

Source: 2008 and 2012: Survey of Working Life; 2016 and 2020: Household Labour Force Survey, Statistics New Zealand.

While official statistics paint a fairly stable picture this doesn't mean that employment insecurity and precarious work are not a considerable problem. Various studies suggest that income volatility can be problematic and that many people feel insecure about their current and future job situations (Moore, 2017; NZCIU, 2013). This is partly related to the exposure of the New Zealand economy to international changes as well as many jobs being seasonal or consumer-flow reliant. For example, the strong pre-Covid growth in tourism and hospitality has been associated with a high turnover of firms and jobs (Mooney et al., 2016; Williamson & Harris, 2019). There has also been considerable recent controversy over employment standards and working time (see below) as employers have tried to limit labour costs and match their staff levels to workflow. This included so-called 'zero hours' employment agreements without set working hours, which became common in some sectors such as hospitality until they were restricted by law changes in 2016 (Campbell, 2018).

Underemployment and what is called underutilisation are also significant labour market issues. The underemployed are part-time employees who would like more work while underutilisation is a broad measure of unemployment that includes the unemployed, the underemployed, those who would like work but are not actively seeking it, and those who are seeking work but are not able to begin work within four weeks. In December 2021, the total number of people classified as underutilised was 277,000 or 9.2% of the extended labour force. This indicates clearly that labour market inclusion is still a considerable problem, despite very low unemployment in 2021. Indeed, underutilisation has been over 10% in most years since 2007. A particular public policy focus has been the number of young people falling outside the wider labour market – young people (15-25 years of age) who are *not* in employment, education and training (NEET). Since the NEET statistics were developed in the early 2000s, there have been more than 10% in this category with a jump to 13%-14% during the Global Financial Crisis.

As in other OECD countries, there has been considerable attention paid to gender issues in New Zealand. The gender pay gap and the low number of female executive and board positions have been roundly criticised in the media and by researchers (Biswas et al., 2021; Tahir, 2016). Although there has been a decline in the gap between male and female earnings over time there is still a considerable gap of nearly 10%. While a number of factors will influence this difference, such as occupational patterns, job position, job tenure and number of hours worked, recent analyses have found that there is a significant gap left which is unexplained by such factors (Pacheco et al., 2019). Although female participation rates and female education achievements have increased in the new millennium there are still many traditional occupations – nursing, teaching, child-care and aged-care – which have predominantly female job holders. These sectors would benefit from the pay equity claims currently unfolding under the Labour Government as pay equity claims could create a similar round of pay rises as those implemented in the aged-care sector in 2017 (see Chapter 4).

Understandably, the gender discussion has been focused on gender imbalances and adverse outcomes for female workers. However, there are also considerable problems amongst working age men. Men tend to score, on average, high in suicides, imprisonment, and low in educational achievements. There are also many job categories where the proportion of men is very low. Interesting, the gender imbalance in educational achievements in favour of women has been bypassed with little media or public policy attention and with hardly any comprehensive attempts to improve the educational achievements of men (Rasmussen & Hannam, 2014). There has also been limited discussion of any links between the female prevalence in education jobs and the inability to address the lower level of educational achievements of boys and young men.

New Zealand has become a multi-cultural society, especially after the high levels of migration during 2012–2018. However, the long-standing labour market issues associated with Māori and Pacific peoples are still dominating official statistics. Māori and Pacific peoples are over-represented when it comes to unemployment (including long-term unemployment), young people not in employment, education and training (NEET), amongst people in seasonal employment and outside the labour force and importantly, amongst people in low paying jobs and occupations.

In the last three decades, the New Zealand population has been 'greying' and people over 60 years of age have become a significant proportion of the working age population. There appears to be two very different trends surrounding older workers. On one hand, there has been a considerable growth in employment participation amongst people over 60 years of age. This started by a lift in eligibility to receive superannuation to 65 years in 2001 but has been driven by other factors since. Besides being associated with older people feeling it financially necessary to keep on working, they may also feel that it is too early to retire. This can partly be associated with improved health and long lifespans. On the other hand, there are many stories about how older people have difficulty in securing another job when they have become redundant or want to re-enter the job market (Poulston, 2016). This is often associated with some form of age discrimination which is clearly unlawful but can also very difficult to detect and prevent.

Immigration and working hours

Following an upswing in migration after the Global Financial Crisis (GFC), immigration has been an important political and labour market issue. As discussed above, there has historically been an influx of migrants into New Zealand to cover skills shortages and this became pronounced during economic upswings. However, the debates were mainly about 'brain drain' and the ethnic mix and skill levels of migrants (Catley, 2001; Small, 2019), though sometimes with xenophobic overtones. The dramatic increase in permanent and temporary migrants in the 2013–2019 period prompted a political reaction and the political parties in the subsequent 2017 Labour-led government promised a reduction in migrant numbers during the 2017 election (Skilling & Molineaux, 2017). However, it lasted until the 2020 Covid-19 pandemic before a dramatic and immediate stop happened to migration. Now, the debates are mainly about when a post-pandemic change to migration can happen and what the new patterns of migration will look like. Will there be a major 'reset' of regulations surrounding migration and if so, what will this 'reset' entail?

Why has it been suggested that a 'reset' of migration levels is necessary? There appears to be little disagreement about the value of permanent, high skill migration to plug specific skills shortages and instead two key arguments in favour of a 'reset' have featured (see Fry & Wilson, 2020). First, the high level of temporary visa holders – estimated to be around 170,000 or 6% of the labour force in 2018 – distorted industry labour markets as some employers adjusted their business models to an availability of 'imported, cheap labour'. This could have encouraged these employers to keep labour costs low and rely on temporary visa holders instead of local labour market employees. Second, it has been argued that "These policies reinforce a low-skill, low wage, low-capital status quo" (Fry & Wilson, 2020: i) and this has negative consequences for productivity growth. As discussed below, New Zealand's productivity levels have languished compared to many other OECD countries and a 'reset' of migration policies could endeavour to enhance productivity growth through encouraging more investments in education and training and in new technology and working practices.

At the time of writing in early 2022, it is unclear whether there will be a significant 'reset' of migration policies and if so, how far this will go and what the consequences will be. So far, some employers have voiced strong concerns about the negative consequences for running their businesses. These are the employers in, for example, horticulture, hospitality, and retail sectors, who have benefited from a strong rise in temporary labour and there have been many media stories of fruit being unpicked and restaurants and retailers cutting opening hours during 2020–2021. Whether this has prompted employers to recruit from local labour markets and raise their wages is rather unclear though it appears to have happened in some parts of horticulture and hospitality. Thus, the theoretical and empirical arguments surrounding migration are likely to feature in the public debate for some time (Conway, 2021).

Working time patterns have been a key labour market issue for several decades. The traditional 40-hour week started to become less prevalent from the 1970s onwards and has covered less than a third of all jobs since the 1990s. The shift towards a post-industrial society and the influx of women in paid work were amongst the key factors driving this change. As mentioned above, a significant number of employees – predominantly women – work part-time. Part-time employment can often facilitate a better work-life balance, but it can also have detrimental career impacts, especially when it involves less than 20 hours a week. Also concerning is the embeddedness of long working hours in New Zealand working patterns. There is now more than one-third of the workforce that usually work more than 40 hours a week and around a quarter works more than 50 hours a week. As a result, Statistics New Zealand has started to record long working hours in 10-hour bands – for example, 60-70 hours a week – up to over 90 hours a week. Thus, the traditional images of 'lazy' New Zealanders and their focus on leisure pursuits have become less true and instead there are concerns that the long working hours have been associated with negative mental and physical well-being effects and with low productivity growth (New Zealand Productivity Commission, 2021; Wong et al., 2019).

Vocational education and training

In recent decades, increased education and vocational training have been seen a key solution in achieving economic success and social inclusion (OECD, 2018; Piercy & Cochrane, 2015). This is most often in reference to the elusive goal of establishing a high wage, high skill, highly productive economy (Rasmussen & Fletcher, 2018). However, there has often been disagreement on *how* to achieve a highly skilled, adaptable workforce to facilitate a high wage, highly productive economy. For example, debate continues over, whether it is the overall skill level or rather skill mismatches that is the problem in the New Zealand labour market.

As discussed in the next section, the recent strong public policy focus on improving productivity growth has yet to bear fruit. While vocational education and training is considered a core part of moving towards higher levels of productivity growth, the persistent disappointing productivity growth in New Zealand raises fundamental questions about education and vocational training systems, including investments in technological skills, and managerial abilities and approaches. In particular, what are the educational and training approaches and levers that will move New Zealand towards being a high wage, highly skilled and highly productive economy?

In the debates about the value of increased education and vocational training, it is often suggested that the future labour market will have fewer low-skilled jobs and that constant upskilling – 'life-long learning' – is necessary to avoid that shortages of skilled people constrain the productive capacity of the economy. While these suggestions appear intuitively plausible with frequent technological innovations, shifting consumer demands and synchronised economic upswing across OECD countries there are currently many service sector jobs with a limited range of technical skill requirements but with an emphasis on 'soft' skills and positive attitudes.

How to achieve a highly skilled, adaptable workforce is influenced by the nature of the national labour market, the kind of institutional support available to lift education and vocational training effort and approaches and attitudes of employers and workers. Comparative research has often lauded the well-established training cultures of Japan, Germany and Sweden with their emphasis on long-life learning and generic skills development. Interestingly, the stronger emphasis on firm-specific skills found in Anglo-American countries can also be considered a competitive advantage.

It is problematic that there appears to be 'fads' in what is currently recommended by international organisations – such as the OECD and the IMF – and there are considerable constraints in transferring positive lessons from one national labour market to other national labour markets (see Bamber et al., 2016). Besides embedded national institutions, there are also the influential attitudes and preferences of policy-makers, interest organisations, employers and workers. These historically developed institutions and attitudes present considerable barriers in transferring the vocational education and training approaches across countries.

Generally, education and vocational training efforts have often been insufficient in New Zealand and in particular, skill developments have had difficulty in keeping up with labour market demands during economic upswings. With a prevalence of small and medium sized businesses (SMEs) there has been a lack of resources and inclination to invest long-term in skill development and, associated with this, there has been a tendency to 'poach' staff from other organisations. Traditionally, the state played a crucial role since it was a major funder of polytechnic institutes and many large public sector organisations had significant apprenticeship and training schemes. While this wasn't sufficient to meet labour market demands during the post-war economic upswing it did provide for a significant provision of skilled employees which were then often 'poached' by private sector employers. This changed dramatically when the so-called 'New Zealand experiment' started to unfold in the late 1980s and early 1990s as public sector reforms and growing unemployment curtailed training efforts (see Chapter 3).

Since the late 1980s, there has been considerable public debate over education and vocational training with dramatic public policy and institutional changes and with a regular re-occurrence of skill shortages and reliance of 'importing labour' (see below for more historical details). In the early 1990s, the National Government continued the neo-liberal 'experiment' by developing a completely new vocational training framework. During 1999–2008, the Labour-led governments continued this framework but introduced Modern Apprenticeships and increased public funding considerably. However, a strong economic upswing put vocational training efforts under considerable pressure until the 2008 Global Financial Crisis.

The 2008–2017 National-led Governments initially reduced investments in vocational education and training but the combination of the Christchurch rebuild after the 2010 earthquake, the 'leaky building' reconstructions and the return of economic growth meant that these governments battled skill shortages in their later years. Most recently, the post-2017 Labour-led Governments have announced a major overhaul of vocational education and training and besides implementing this major policy overhaul, the current government is also faced with a major re-balancing of the national economy after the fall-out from the COVID-19 pandemic.

Historical changes to vocational education and training policies

The 1992 Industry Training Act was part of the neo-liberal political 'experiment' and presented a radical different way of enhancing vocational training as well as introducing a completely new qualification framework. While there was widespread agreement on enhancing flexibility and portability of skill attainment, as well as meeting new training demands from the growing service sectors there was considerable disagreement about the Act's reliance on market forces to provide sufficient and suitable training development (see Table 9.3 in Rasmussen, 2009: 252). The new Industry Training Organisations (ITOs) gave primacy to the employers' role in highlighting and reacting to skill demands, government funding was initially very limited, and many employers had difficulty in navigating the new qualification framework. With subdued economic conditions and a radical new employment relations system many employers had little inclination to invest in training during the early to mid 1990s (see Chapter 3).

From the start of the Industry Training Act there were critical comments regarding its confusing growth of ITOs and qualifications as well as its ability to overcome traditional training weaknesses, including SMEs' ability and willingness to invest in training. The new vocational education and training system also had to compensate for the downturn in training efforts prior and during the introduction of the new framework. By the mid-1990s, there were over 50 ITOs – equivalent to roughly 10 times the number of ITOs in Australia when measured in terms of employee numbers – and growing concerns about their efficiency and duplication of training efforts. Thus, the government had to deal with a fine-tuning of the new system as well as ramping up training efforts. In late 1990s, this led to an increase in public funding and constant pressure on ITOs to amalgamate and collaborate better with existing providers such as polytechnic institutes.

The 1999–2008 Labour-led governments came into power with

promises of doing much better in vocational education and training. Prior to the 1999 general election, the Labour Party had promised a strong increase in public funding, a rise in training efforts and their coverage and in particular, the development of a Modern Apprenticeship scheme to increase the number of young people in apprenticeships. Interestingly, the Labour-led Governments kept most of the existing structures and tried instead to make the vocational training approach more efficient by facilitating ITO amalgamations, improve ITO-polytechnic institute collaborations and encourage employers to take on apprentices through the provision of education co-ordinators to manage apprenticeship paperwork.

With a strong economic upswing during 2002–2008 (see Chapter 4), there were rampant skill shortages, and the government quadrupled its vocation training funding during 1999–2008 (Collins, 2012). In line with its overall political philosophy the government also encouraged tripartite collaborations as exemplified by the 2008 Skill Strategy for New Zealand (Tertiary Education Commission, 2008). While official statistics showed a strong rise in university degrees, trainee numbers and vocational qualification completions this was insufficient and a kind of 'catch-up' was continuously being played in respect of labour market demands. Until the Global Financial Crisis in 2008, the new job vacancy surveys and statistics created by Department of Labour recorded unsatisfied demand in a wide range of occupations and jobs (Silverstone & Wall, 2008).

The 2008–2017 National-led governments were faced immediately with a major economic upheaval because of the Global Financial Crisis. As well, the Christchurch earthquakes and the 'leaking buildings' debacle created unprecedented demands in the construction industry. Interestingly, the government allowed vocational training to decline from 133,000 to 83,000 trainees during 2008–2011 (Collins, 2012). This decline is also recorded in Figure 6.2 and it created a considerable pent-up demand as construction projects took off and the economy improved. As a reaction, the government allowed considerable 'import' of workers and immigration soared to historically unprecedented levels with net migration peaking at over 60,000 in 2016–2018 (as discussed above). Extra funding was also allocated to vocational training providers and the government started to incentivise employers to take on apprentices. This resulted in training efforts and trainee numbers stabilising during 2015–2017.

Figure 6.2 Participants in industry training, 1995–2019

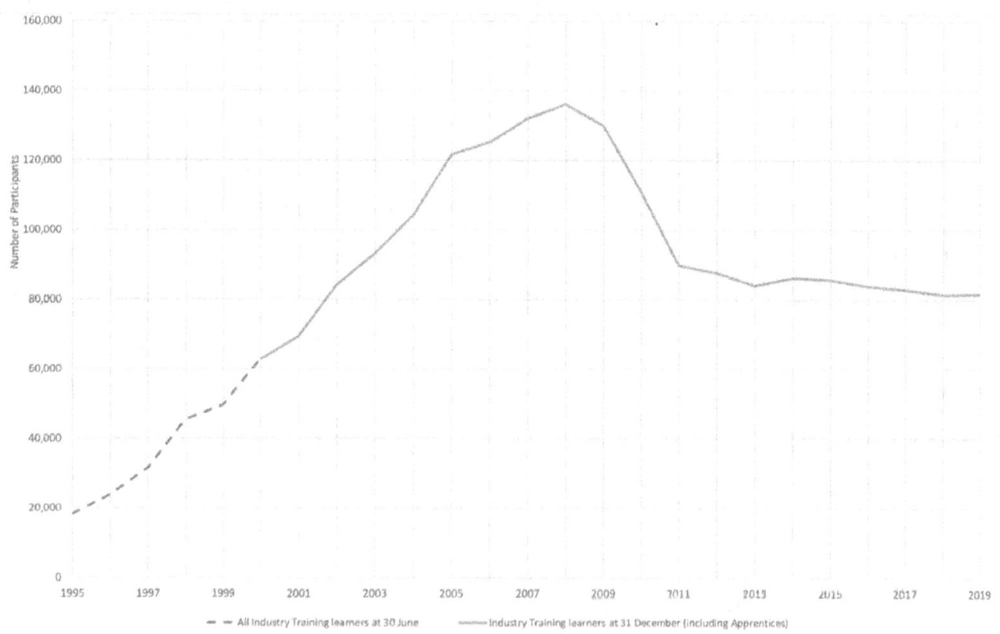

Source: Participation Industry Training 2020, Education Counts.

https://www.educationcounts.govt.nz/statistics/vocational-education-and-training

Note: Counts from 2000 may not be comparable with previous years because of changes to reporting systems.

Like the previous Labour-led Governments, the National-led Governments' training efforts were continuously playing 'catch-up', despite the unprecedented high level of net immigration during 2013–2017. During this period, a number of policy packages were announced. The first policy measure was the industry training review (2011–2012) that placed the performance of ITOs under scrutiny and led to operational reforms in 2013. The second key policy measure was the 2014 amendment to the Industry Training Act that removed the modern apprenticeship and trainee schemes and replaced them with New Zealand Apprenticeships (NZAs). Trades Academies were launched alongside NZAs' scholarship scheme and were established in Secondary Schools, Polytechnics and Private Training Establishments (Piercy & Cochrane, 2015). Targeted reviews of qualifications were also undertaken by the New Zealand Qualifications Authority to reduce duplication and the Vocational Pathways initiative for career advice was established.

Another important policy package was Better Public Services. This initiative included the target to "Increase the proportion of 25 to 34-year-olds with advanced trade qualifications, diplomas and degrees (at level 4 or above) to 55%." (New Zealand Government, 2012). Despite the overall inability to match demand for skilled labour, there were some improvements with fewer ITOs (falling from 38 in 2007 to 12 in 2017), a stronger focus on qualification completion rates, creating clearer career pathways for school leavers and establishing an annual occupational outlook to guide young people and other decision-makers.

The 2017 Labour-led Government came into office with promises of significant improvements in the funding of education and vocational training. The Labour Party's promise of three years of fee-free post-school study across a person's lifetime became initially a one-year fee-free study right. The capital investments in schools were combined with a significant rise in funding as the government increased teachers' salaries considerably, following several rounds of industrial disputes. Most importantly, the Government announced a radical overhaul of vocational education and training in 2019. The Reform of Vocational Education (RoVE) – based on the Education (Vocational Education and Training Reform) Amendment Act in April 2020 – was the biggest change since the Industry Training Act 1992. As detailed below, it involved new strategies, structures, funding mechanisms and education processes (see Figure 6.3).

Given the magnitude of the changes, the reform process was designed to give Polytechnics and Industry Training Organisations a three-year period to fully enact the reform process. The RoVE changes created Te Pukenga (NZ Institute of Skills and Technology) by merging 16 Polytechs (so-called Industry Training Providers – ITPs). This national organisation was responsible for supporting both workplace-based (on-job) training, and classroom-based (off-job) training. As such, some of the functions of ITOs will transition into this organisation. However, the merger process will not conclude until 2022 and, in the meantime, ITOs are currently operating as Transitional Industry Training Organisations.

Aspects of the ITO system will also contribute to six Workforce Development Councils that cover the vocational pathway sectors of:

1. Manufacturing, Engineering and Logistics;
2. Construction and Infrastructure;
3. Creative, Cultural, Recreation and Technology;
4. Health, Community and Social Services;
5. Service Industries;
6. Primary Industries.

The main function of the Workforce Development Councils is to develop national skills leadership plans to shape and inform the direction for workforce and qualification development for their respective industries. This has now been aligned with the government's plans for industry partnership to develop transformational strategies.

Other organisations created by these reforms include Centres of Vocational Excellence, and Te Taumata Aronui (a group designed to ensure the reforms reflect the Government's commitment to Māori Crown partnerships) that sits alongside the governance structure for Te Pukenga. The Ministry of Business, Innovation and Employment is also responsible for regional skills leadership groups (RSLGs) that are governance bodies similar to Workforce Development Councils but their focus is on developing regional strategies for skills development. Overall, Te Pūkenga has 17 subsidiary organisations which provide vocational education and training throughout New Zealand. The subsidiaries are governed by Boards of Directors appointed by Te Pūkenga's Council.

This is what the new system will look like:

Figure 6.3 Model of new vocation, education and training system

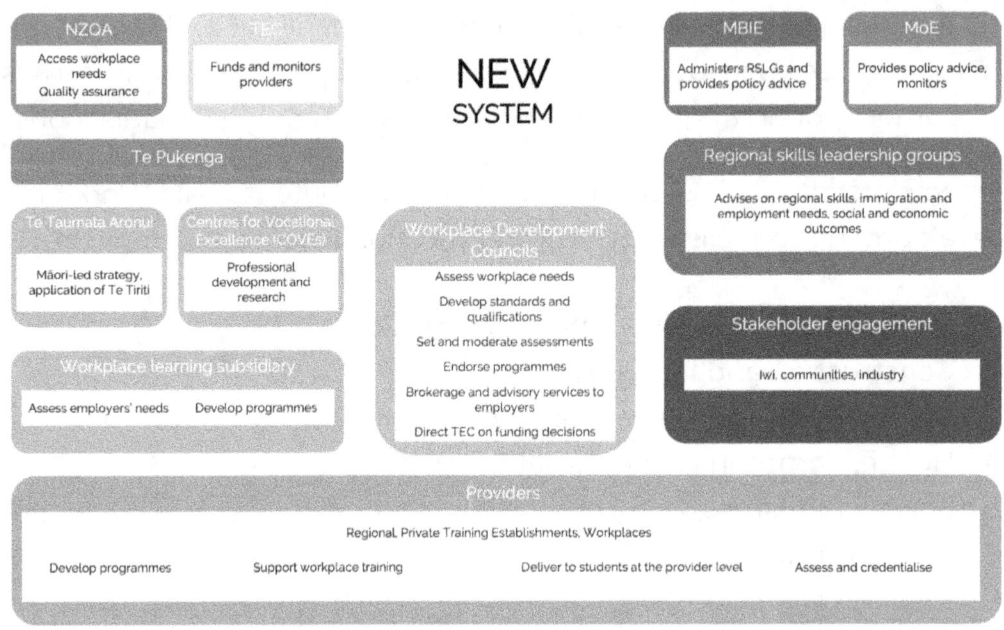

Source: Piercy-Cameron, 2022 (adapted from other available figures)

The radical reshaping of vocational education and training started just as the Covid-19 pandemic hit New Zealand. Skills development has been put forward as a solution to the unemployment and labour market dislocation caused by the pandemic. As such the reform process in relation to the WDCs and RSLGs has been accelerated. The government has also created a new policy initiative launched in July 2020 that fully funds sub-degree qualifications at levels 3-7 on the qualifications framework (Tertiary Education Commission, 2020). Uptake has been significant with more than 100,000 signing up for free vocational training courses and as well, in tandem with this change, a Southern Auckland initiative has focused on increased trades participation amongst Māori and Pasifika (for details, see Piercy & Rasmussen, 2022).

Despite these positive moves some of the involved organisations – especially some Polytechs and ITOs – have voiced their concerns over the potential fallouts for individual organisations and the overall ability of the new system to deliver quality education and training (Competenz, 2019). So far, the uptake of trades students appears to have addressed these potential fallouts, but it is happening in a situation where skills and labour shortages caused by border closure is putting the government under political pressure (see above). Interestingly, employers appear to be mainly positive about the changes and there has also been union support. Whether the lack of employer criticism has been overshadowed by the economic and industry disruption caused by the pandemic will probably first become clear when RoVE is fully implemented and the disruption of the pandemic is in the past.

Thus, at the time of writing, there is another major change happening in vocational education and training – on par with the 1990s changes – amidst economic rebuilding following the Covid-19 pandemic. While it has become a mantra that continuous skill developments should be an ingrained part of economic success and social inclusion there is a lack of clarity of how best to facilitate adequate skill development. This has clearly been the case in New Zealand where economic upswings and tight labour markets are associated with skill shortages and the 'import' of workers. Constantly, training efforts have lagged behind labour market demands and, besides belated investments in vocational education and training, various schemes have tried to alleviate labour shortfalls in many key industries, such as agriculture and horticulture, tourism and hospitality, construction and IT sectors.

The perennial problem of weak productivity growth

Productivity and rising productivity levels have become crucial measures of the relative success of national economies and their economic performance. As Nobel Prize Winner Paul Krugman has famously coined it: "Productivity isn't everything, but, in the long run, it is almost everything. A country's ability to improve its standard of living over time depends almost entirely on its ability to raise its output per worker." (Krugman, 1994: 11). It has become, therefore, of considerable concern that New Zealand's relative productivity growth has been dismal over many decades (Conway & Meehan, 2013; NZ Productivity Commission, 2016).

This has raised many questions and issues in respect of how to lift New Zealand's productivity performance but there has been less success in providing sustainable improvements in actual productivity growth. Interestingly, the major employment relations framework changes in the last three to four decades have been driven partly by an attempt to lift productivity levels (see Chapters 3 & 4). Still, it has also been questioned recently whether legislative employment relations reforms in themselves can raise productivity performance significantly (Peetz, 2012; Rasmussen & Fletcher, 2018).

Discussions of productivity growth have been around for a long time and its basic conceptualisation – producing more value through using input resources better – is well-known economic territory (see Conway, 2016; NZ Productivity Commission, 2021). In basic terms, productivity drivers are: investments in physical and human capital, innovation and investments in research and development, competition pressures, superior workplace relationships and skill utilisation. Or as the NZ Productivity Commission (2021: 3) has formulated it, productivity can be lifted by "producing more with what we have (people, knowledge, skills, produced capital, and natural resources)."

However, productivity is also a tricky concept fraught with measurement problems and the literature will often use at least two different key measures: labour productivity and multifactor productivity. Labour productivity is normally understood as goods and services produced per worker or per hour worked and is measured as developments in output divided by labour input (Gross Domestic Product (GDP) per capita). Multifactor productivity is a broader concept that measures the amount of output produced by taking into account all the inputs used, including labour, capital, land and intermediate goods or raw materials. It therefore captures the efficiency with which all factors together are used to produce the outputs.

There are different views about the most successful ways for a country to achieve higher productivity growth. While the NZ Productivity Commission (2021: 38-42) points to the usual factors and especially highlights the role of innovation it is unclear exactly how it will happen that New Zealand "produces more with what we have". There are stark differences between, for example, a neo-liberal approach of reduced state intervention, lower taxes, deregulation, and employer-driven flexibility and a social-democratic approach of considerable state intervention, high taxes, strong regulatory measures (often including support of collective bargaining), and comprehensive employee rights and protections.

Table 6.4 Sector level productivity over cycles

		Measured sector	Primary industries	Goods producing industries	Service industries	Education & training	Healthcare and social assistance	Public admin & safety
1997–2000	LP	2.9	-0.4	3.2	3.3	-1.3	5.6	
	MFP	1.9	-0.4	2	2.2	-1.9	5.1	
2000–2008	LP	1.3	2.1	0.6	1.7	-1.5	0.8	
	MFP	0.6	0.3	0.1	0.9	-1.7	0.5	
2008–2018	LP	1	2	0.4	1.1	-1.3	-0.3	
	MFP	0.6	0.7	0	0.7	-1.6	-0.3	
1996–2018	LP	1.4	2.3	0.9	1.5	-1.4	0.8	
	MFP	0.8	0.9	0.3	0.9	-1.7	0.5	
Employment share	1996	82.6	11.3	26	45.3	5.8	6.6	5
	2018	77.9	6.9	22.3	48.7	7.3	9.1	5.6

Source: New Zealand Productivity Commission, 2019.

Note: LP = Labour Productivity; MFP = Multifactor Productivity.

As discussed in Chapters 3 and 4, the ECA 1991 was based on a very different understanding of achieving higher productivity growth than the ERA 2000. As well as these differences, there are a myriad of different combinations of public policy approaches and workplace practices which could be used to target higher economy-wide productivity growth rates, as well as continuous debates of whether regulatory measures are synchronised and supportive of each other (Haworth, 2010). This could include much stronger regulatory support for the role of unions and collective bargaining beyond the Employment Relations Act 2000, such as Fair Pay Agreements and union membership becomes an automatic option (see Harcourt et al., 2020; Kent, 2021).

As can be seen from Table 6.4, there has been downward trend overall in both labour productivity and multifactor productivity growth rates in the last three productivity cycles. The agriculture sector has shown the strongest growth, due in part to changes in land use and the shift to dairying. (Note that productivity as measured here does not capture negative environmental impacts such as water quality and greenhouse gas emissions.)

Figure 6.4 GDP per capita as a percentage of the OECD mean (US$ PPPs)

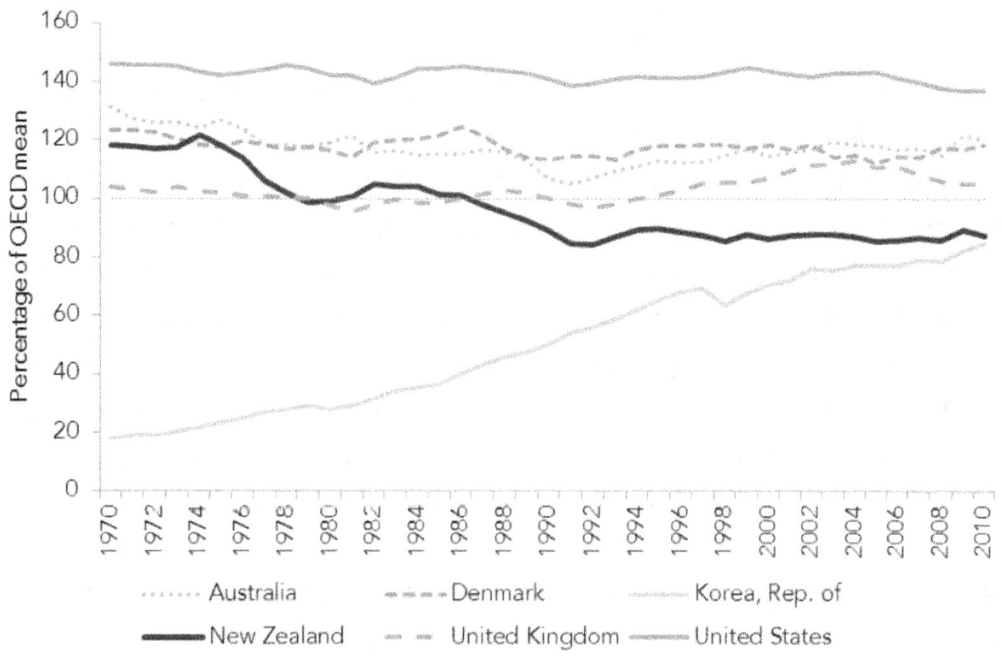

Source: Conway and Meehan, 2013, p.23

This downward trend is reflected in New Zealand's declining *relative* productivity performance in respect to most other OECD countries (see Figure 6.4). This relative decline has been particularly important in respect of Australia where GDP per hour worked in New Zealand has dropped to less than 70% of that in Australia (after being on or above 100% in the 1960s). Or as formulated by Rasmussen and Fletcher (2018: 78): "though neither country can be pleased about their productivity growth it is clear that New Zealand's productivity performance is at a different and much more concerning level."

Thus, there is little disagreement that New Zealand needs to improve its productivity performance. The poor productivity growth has been described as a 'paradox' by international and domestic researchers based on their belief that the opening of the economy, wide-ranging deregulation, and decentralised workplace bargaining in the 1980s and 1990s would lift productivity growth levels (de Serres et al., 2014). However, it became clear in the second half of the 1990s that, despite some positive impact from job shedding and work intensification, there had not been a fundamental shift in productivity levels.

The disappointing productivity levels of the 1990s indicated that the public policy approach and reliance on more market-orientated solutions had been insufficient. Instead, it was argued that it would be necessary to pursue *either* stronger market-orientated interventions (as suggested by the Business Roundtable, see Kerr, 2008) *or* move in another direction with the state ensuring larger investments in infrastructure, training and development and new technology combined with more incentives for employers to enhance workplace productivity measures. The latter was clearly the opinion of the 1999–2008 Labour-led Governments (Wilson, 2004) which also shifted completely the view of collective bargaining and union activity from being perceived as barriers to being seen in a positive light (see Chapter 4). There were also specific initiatives such as the Workplace Productivity Group and the Workplace Partnership Centre. While these initiatives had some impact in the public sector and individual workplaces it had limited success in lifting national productivity performance in the 1999–2008 period (Haworth, 2010).

While the key tenets of the ERA were kept in place under the 2008–2017 National-led Governments there was a reversal towards an emphasis on employer-driven flexibility. There was also increased pressure on government funding prompted by the Global Financial Crises and the Christchurch earthquakes. The policy determined drive to secure a balanced budget meant that there was again a shortfall of investments in infrastructure, training and development and public sector services. This started to change in the National-led Government's last years, including a significant lift in wages of age-care workers (see Chapter

4). A Productivity Commission was also established in 2012 and in the following years, it produced a string of reports on productivity issues, measures and potential barriers (for example, see Conway & Meehan, 2013; NZ Productivity Commission, 2019, 2021). However, the public policy influence of these reports appears to have been limited so far.

Thus, there have been significant changes in economic and labour market policies over the last three to four decades to lift labour market performance and productivity levels. In particular, the last two major legislative employment relations frameworks have been seeking to enhance productivity levels. As Table 6.4 and Figure 6.4 show, these reforms appear to have had limited impact and the search for stronger productivity growth – preferably stronger than most other OECD countries – is ongoing.

Following several decades of lacklustre productivity growth, there have been many different arguments about the reasons behind the inability to raise productivity levels, including the possible limited *influence of legislative employment relations reforms* (see Rasmussen & Fletcher, 2018). Interestingly, the influence of employment relations is less prevalent in the current debate as the most prevalent explanatory factors mentioned are: inadequate investments in infrastructure, new technology, research and workforce upskilling, 'remoteness' from key markets, insufficient managerial capabilities and approaches, short-termism and limited policy synergies, employment growth in low-productivity jobs, and overseas ownership or control of key economic activities (New Zealand Productivity Commission, 2019).

In short, there are many explanatory factors being raised. Interestingly, the current focus has moved away from the perceived negative influence of unions and collective bargaining and instead the focus is more on what employers and managers can do to increase productivity growth. Business strategies and behaviours are now being seen as problematic because many employers and sectors have become reliant on low paid workers, 'poaching', and 'import of labour'. The current Labour Government seeks to encourage employers to move away from high labour utilisation and instead invest more in labour-saving, productivity-increasing technology and work practices (see above the current debate about immigration and 'importing' labour). While this has included more emphasis on stronger labour standards, higher statutory minima and increased vocational training efforts it is unclear whether this will overcome an inefficient reliance on 'cheap labour'. Likewise, following the economic upheaval prompted by the Covid-19 pandemic it is debatable, as discussed above, whether this will provide a major economic and employment relations 'reset' or a continuation of the historical low productivity growth path.

Workplace change, partnerships and employee participation structures

There has been a long-term interest in employee participation and influence and this interest has increased with modern human resource management approaches where employee 'buy-in' or commitment is often seen as crucial for highly innovative and productive workplaces (Macky, 2018). However, there are at least *three* fundamental problems with this basic positive understanding of employee participation, influence and commitment.

First, it is often not specified in detail how this positive link to innovative and productive workplaces will actually take place as it assumes particular managerial and employee attitudes and behaviours (Caraker et al., 2016; Iqbal, 2019). Second, it is unclear how employee participation and influence is aligned with notion of managerial prerogative: does it assume a dilution of managerial prerogative and if so, how much dilution would such a rise in employee participation entail? Third, there are many different concepts applied – often indiscriminately – in the discussion of employee participation where it is unclear whether we are talking about: voluntary or legislative backed participation, direct or indirect (though a representative) participation, financial or nonfinancial participation (see Budd, 2014; Caraker et al., 2016; Rasmussen, 2009: 495-7).

There have been similar problems in the New Zealand debate and the concepts of employee participation, influence and commitment and their implementations are surrounded by controversy and a variety of understandings. While employers have been keen to promote more employment commitment of a voluntary nature there have also been several attempts to promote both union backed participation schemes and legislative backed participation structures. In the following, we will address these three different types of employee participation.

The managerial promotion of employee participation has often aligned with progressive human management approaches where employee involvement can have positive effects on organisational performance. There are, however, a number of assumptions associated with positive effects (see Ababneh & Macky, 2015) as well as demanding comprehensive and sustained management efforts (Newman & Freilekhman, 2020). Earlier New Zealand research has highlighted some positive management efforts to institute voluntary, low level participation mechanisms (see Boxall et al., 2007) though it is unclear whether these efforts are widespread currently. Still, recent literature has pointed to the importance of employee engagement, well-being and employee retention as underpinning organisational performance (Bailey et al., 2017; Edgar et al., 2018; Iqbal, 2019). This is particular the case in tight labour markets where the competition for skilled, talented and engaged employees often can be fierce and this has been the case in several industries during the post-2000 years in New Zealand.

Union backed schemes date as far back as the Second World War but there have mainly been two versions in recent decades: Workplace Reform in the 1990s and Workplace Partnerships in the 2000s. Workplace Reform started in the late 1980s, but it really gained traction when a tripartite organisation Workplace New Zealand was set up in 1991 (Perry et al., 1995). This organisation organised two large conferences in 1992 and 1996 and it supported and published information about workplace reform initiatives in New Zealand and overseas (Rasmussen, 2009: 479-482). While some major companies were involved in various workplace changes there was not broad-based support and some employers and unions were either ambivalent or against such collaborative efforts (Chong et al., 2001).

Workplace Partnerships were initially a public sector initiative promoted by the Public Sector Association (PSA). It received support through the Partnership Resource Centre which sponsored research and workplace interventions, including using nominated consultants (Rasmussen & Tedestedt, 2017). While the expected increase in collective bargaining did not occur under the ERA 2000 (see Chapter 4) there were several interesting workplace initiatives, especially in the public sector. However, Workplace Partnerships had difficulty in surviving the shift in government post-2008 and, besides a few organisations continuing their efforts, Workplace Partnerships started to disappear after the Global Financial Crisis. Whether this approach will be resurrected under the current Labour Government is still unclear.

There have been several attempts to institute legislative prescribed participation schemes and structures. Such schemes are different in nature since employers and managers have less say in their form and implementation. These schemes align with statutory employment minima but are different since small and medium size employers are often exempt. For example, the 1989 report of the Committee of Enquiry into Industrial Democracy proposed joint consultative committees in enterprises with 40 or more employees. However, the proposal sank without trace since it hardly featured in public policy debates of the time, it had limited union support, and employers preferred a voluntary approach (Deeks, 1990; Newman & Freilekhman, 2020; Rasmussen & Tedestedt, 2017).

The introduction of legislation backed occupational health and safety (OHS) committees in 2002 as part of the Health and Safety in Employment Amendment Act was a decisive step forward (see Chapter

5). These committees gave employee a legal right to elect health and safety representatives in organisations with 30 or more employees. This was further extended in the Health and Safety at Work Act 2015 where OHS committees were mandated in organisations with 20 or more employees. While there have been suggestions that OHS committees could be an integral part of more productive employment relationships (Lamm, 2010) there is little broadly based research evidence to support such claims and it is contradicted by New Zealand's dismal health and safety record (Lilley et al., 2013; Pashorina-Nichols, 2016). It was acknowledged by Rasmussen and Tedestedt (2017: 184) that

> ...one can only wonder why the various governments and academic researchers have yet to put major efforts into evaluating employee participation in OHS. It is also interesting to note that some of the preliminary research findings show an uneven pattern across employers and their willingness to implement participatory process.

Overall, the three different approaches have disappointed in their extension and implementation though this is clearly an area where more research is needed. The voluntary schemes promoted by employers have seldom moved beyond informative and low level consultation. Across New Zealand organisations a variety of schemes has been tried but there is limited evidence available to evaluate the current dominant schemes and their impact. Interestingly, there appears to have been few financial participation schemes beyond traditional performance payment schemes and neither is there a New Zealand tradition for having tax inducements. With the decline in union strength, there have been few union-backed participation schemes and the Workplace Reform and Workplace Partnership attempts have had limited reach beyond particular firms and public sector organisations. While legislative mandated OHS committees have constituted something of a break-through in respect of legislative schemes their wider and specific workplace impacts have been unclear.

Conclusion

New Zealand employment relations have been through major changes but the longevity of the ERA 2000 has started to settle 'things' after the dramatic changes unleashed by the ECA 1991. The post-2000 reforms have made important changes to workplace employment relations – as described in Chapters 4 and 5 – but the main pillars of the ERA 2000 are still there and it is possible to establish key areas of change and disagreement.

This chapter is less about the ERA 2000 than its surrounding public policies and what employers, unions, employees and self-employed have agreed or accepted. These working standards are shifted by legislation about employment standards, pay equity and statutory minima as well as by societal norms, regulatory enforcement and media reports. It is an adjustment, however, that can often be rather slow and this is probably one of the reasons why the 'low wage, low skill, low productivity' and gender, ethnicity and age differences have become embedded issues. On that background, short-term adjustments are seldom about wholesale changes but rather about the direction (positive or negative) of changes.

Likewise, it is crucial to detect whether there have been shifts in the employment relations narrative and how it is envisaged that employment relations improvements can be brought about. The lingering of the neo-liberal, free-market approaches of the 1980s and 1990s can still be detected but there have been considerable adjustments to the thinking and narrative of key employment relations actors in the new millennium. In particular, stronger regulatory interventions have featured across a number of public policy areas as discussed above in respect of labour market inclusion (gender, ethnicity, age), vocational education and training, low wages, and OHS committees. It is also expected that there will be considerable change associated with how the economic and employment fall-outs of the 2020 and 2021 Covid-19 'lockdowns' are and will be tackled.

References

Ababneh, O. & Macky, K. (2015). The meaning and measurement of employee engagement: A review of the literature. *New Zealand Journal of Human Resource Management*, 15(1), 1-35.

Anderson, P., & Warhurst, C. (2012). Lost in translation? Skills policy and the shift to skill ecosystems. In T. Dolphin and T. Nash (Eds.), *Complex New World: Translating new economic theory into public policy* (pp. 109-120). Institute for Public Policy Research.

Bailey, C., Madden, A., Alfes, K. & Fletcher, L. (2017). The meaning, antecedents and autcomes of employment engagement: A narrative synthesis. *International Journal of Management Reviews*, 19, 31-53.

Bamber, G. J., Lansbury R. D., Wailes, N., & Wright C. F. (2016). *International and comparative employment relations: National regulation, global changes.* (6th edition). Allen and Unwin.

Bell, D. 1974. *The Coming of the Post-industrial Society.* Heinemann.

Biswas, P.B., Roberts, H. & Stainback, K. (2021). Does women's board representation affect non-managerial gender inequality? *Human Resource Management*, 60(4), 659-680. https://doi.org/10.1002/hrm.22066

Blackwood, K., Bentley, T., Green, N. & Tappin, D. (2018). Changing terrain: Flexible forms of working and their meaning for human resource management and employment relations. In Parker, J. & Baird, M. (Eds.), *The Big Issues in Employment* (pp. 51-72). Wolters Kluwer.

Boxall, P., Haynes, P. & Macky, K. (2007). Employee voice and voicelessness in New Zealand. In Freeman, R., Boxall, P. & Haynes, P. (Eds.), *What workers say: Employee voice in the Anglo-American workplace* (pp. 145-165). Cornell University Press.

Budd, J. (2014). The future of employee voice. In Wilkinson, A.,

Donaghey, J., Dundon, T. & Freeman, R. (Eds.), *The handbook of research in employee voice* (pp. 477-488). Edward Elgar.

Campbell, I. (2018). Zero-hour work arrangements in New Zealand: Union action, public controversy and two regulatory initiatives. In O'Sullivan, M., Lavelle, J., McMahon, J., Ryan, L., Murphy, C., Turner, T. & Gunnigle, P. (Eds.), *Zero hours and on-call work in Anglo-Saxon countries* (pp. 91-110). Springer.

Caraker, E., Jøregensen, H., Madsen, M.O. & Baadsgaard, K. (2016). Representation without co-determination? *Economic and Industrial Democracy, 37*(2), 269-295.

Catley, B. (2001). The New Zealand 'brain drain'. *People and Place,* 9(3), 54-65.

Chong, K.P. Mealings, A. & Rasmussen, E. (2001). *Giving voice to the employee: Employee perspectives of workplace reform in New Zealand.* Paper, Department of Management and Employment Relations, University of Auckland.

Collins, S. (2012). Getting more bang out of our trade education buck. *New Zealand Herald,* 21 November 2012, pp. A18-A19.

Competenz. (2019). Vocational education reform 'devastating' for NZ industry. 19 March 2019. https://www.competenz.org.nz/news/vocational-education-reform-devastating-for-nz-industry/

Conway, P. (2016). *Achieving New Zealand's productivity potential.* Research Paper 2016/1, New Zealand Productivity Commission.

Conway, P. (2021). Time for the migration conversation. *Sunday Star-Times,* 4 July 2021, p. 62.

Conway, P. & Meehan, L. (2013). *Productivity by the numbers: The New Zealand experience.* Research Paper 2013/1. New Zealand Productivity Commission.

Deeks, J.S. (1990). New tracks, old maps: continuity and change in New

Zealand labour relations 1984-1990. *New Zealand Journal of Industrial Relations*, 15(2), 99-116.

de Serres, A., Yashiro, N. & Boulohol, H. (2014). *An international perspective on the New Zealand productivity paradox.* New Zealand Productivity Commission.

Edgar, F., Geare, A. & Zhang, J.A. (2018). Accentuating the positive: The mediating role of positive emotions in the HRM-contextual performance relationship. *International Journal of Manpower*, 39(7), 954-970.

Foster, B. & Rasmussen, E. (2017). The major parties: National's and Labour's employment relations policies. *New Zealand Journal of Employment Relations*, 42(2), 95-109.

Fry, J. & Wilson, P. (2021). *Could do better. Migration and New Zealand's frontier firms.* Report commissioned by the NZ Productivity Commission, NZIER, September 2021.

Groot, S., van Ommen, C., Masters-Awatere, B., & Tassell-Matamua, N. (2017). *Precarity: Uncertain, insecure and unequal lives in Aotearoa New Zealand.* Massey University Press.

Harcourt, M., Gall, G., Wilson, M., Rubenstein, K. & Shang, S. (2020). Public support for a union defailt: Predicting factors and implications for public policy. *Economic and Industrial Democracy*, https://doi-org.ezproxy.aut.ac.nz/10.1177/0143831X20969811

Haworth, N. (2010). Economic transformation, productivity and employment relations in New Zealand 1999–2008. In Rasmussen, E. (ed.). *Employment relationships: workers, unions and employers in New Zealand* (pp. 149-167). Auckland University Press.

Iqbal, M. (2019). *High-involvement work processes, trust and employee engagement: The mediating role of perceptions of organisational justice and politics.* PhD Thesis, Auckland University of Technology.

Kent, A. (2021). New Zealand's Fair Pay Agreements: A new direction in sectoral and occupational bargaining. *Labour & Industry* 31(3), 235-254. https://doi.org/10.1080/10301763.2021.1910899

Kerr, R. (2008). Closing gaps needs change of direction. NZ Herald, 28 April 2008, p. C2.

Krugman, P. (1994). *The Age of Diminished Expectations*. MIT Press.

Lamm, F. (2010). Participative and productive employment relations: the role of health and safety committees and worker representation. In Rasmussen, E. (ed.). *Employment relationships: workers, unions and employers in New Zealand* (pp. 168-184). Auckland University Press.

Lilley, R., Samaranayaka, A. & Weiss, H. (2013). *International comparison of International Labour Organization published occupational fatal injury rates: How does New Zealand compare internationally?* Commissioned report for the Independent Taskforce on Workplace Health and Safety. http://hstaskforce.govt.nz/working-papers.asp

Macky, K. (2018). Strategic people management – Where have we come from and where are we going? In Parker, J. & Baird, M. (Eds.), *The Big Issues in Employment* (pp. 203-223). Wolters Kluwer.

Mooney, S., Harris, C. & Ryan, I. (2016). Long hospitality career – A contradiction in terms? *International Journal of Contemporary Hospitality Management*, 28(11), 2589-2608.

Moore, T. (2017). Income volatility in New Zealand. *Policy Quarterly*, 13(4), 44-52.

Newman, A. & Freilekhman, I. (2020). A case for regulatory industrial democracy post Covid-19. *New Zealand Journal of Employment Relations*, 42(2), 70-76.

NZCTU. (2013). *Under pressure: A detailed report into insecure work in New Zealand*. NZ Council of Trades Unions.

New Zealand Government. (2012). Better public services results: Targets and public communication Cabinet paper. [CAB (12) 315]. https://www.publicservice.govt.nz/our-work/better-public-services/

New Zealand Productivity Commission. (2019). *Technological change and the future of work.* https://www.productivity.govt.nz/inquiries/ technology-and-the-future-of-work/

New Zealand Productivity Commission. (2021). *Productivity by the numbers: 2019.* www.productivity.govt.nz/productivity-by-the-numbers/

New Zealand Productivity Commission. (2020). *Research Publications.* www.productivity.govt.nz/research

OECD. (2018). *Opportunities for all: A framework for policy action on inclusive growth.* https://www.oecd-ilibrary.org/

OECD. (2019). *OECD economic survey of New Zealand.* OECD Publishing.

Pacheco, G., Li, C. & Cochrane, B. (2019). An empirical examination of the gender pay gap in New Zealand. *New Zealand Journal of Employment Relations*, 44(1), 1-20.

Pashorina-Nichols, V. (2016). Occupational health and safety: Why and how should worker participation be enhanced in New Zealand? *New Zealand Journal of Employment Relations*, 41(2), 71-86.

Peetz, D. (2012). Does Industrial Relations Policy Affect Productivity? *Australian Bulletin of Labour*, 38(4), 268-292.

Perry, M., Davidson, C. & Hill, R. (1995). *Reform at Work.* Longman Paul.

Piercy, G., & Cochrane, B. (2015). The skills productivity disconnect: Aotearoa New Zealand industry training policy post-2008 election. *New Zealand Journal of Employment Relations*, 40(1), 53-69.

Piercy, G. & Rasmussen, E. (2022, February 8-10). Vocational education and training reforms before, under and beyond the Covid-19 pandemic.

[Paper presentation]. New Zealand Political Studies Association conference, Auckland.

Poulston, J. (2016). Barriers to the employment of older hotel workers in New Zealand. *Journal of Human Resources in Hospitality and Tourism*, 15(1), 45-68.

Rasmussen, E. & Fletcher, M. (2018). Employment relations reforms and New Zealand's 'productivity paradox'. *Australian Journal of Labour Economics*, 21(1), 75-92.

Rasmussen, E. & Hannam, B. (2014). Before and beyond the Great Financial Crisis: Men and education, labour market and well-being trends and issues in New Zealand. *New Zealand Journal of Employment Relations*, 38(3), 24-33.

Rasmussen, E. & Tedestedt, R. (2017). Waves of interest in employee participation in New Zealand. In Anderson, G., Geare, A., Rasmussen, E. & Wilson, M. (Eds.), *Transforming workplace relations 1976-2016* (pp. 169-190). Victoria University Press.

Silverstone, B. & Wall, V. (2008). *Job vacancy monitoring in New Zealand.* [Paper presentation]. Labour, Employment and Work Conference, Wellington. https://ojs.victoria.ac.nz/LEW/article/view/1660

Skilling, P. & Molineaux, J. (2017). New Zealand's minor parties and ER policy after 2017. *New Zealand Journal of Employment Relations*, 42(2), 110-128.

Small, Z. (2019, July 8). Statistics New Zealand no longer measuring 'brain drain' to Australia. *Newshub.* https://www.newshub.co.nz/home/politics/2019/03/statistics-new-zealand-no-longer-measuring-brain-drain-to-australia.html

Stewart, A. & Stanford, J. (2017). Regulating work in the gig economy: What are the options? *Economic and Labour Relations Review*, 28(3), 420-437.

Tahir, R. (2016). Does gender matter? Female representation on the corporate boards: The case study of New Zealand. *International Journal of Management Development*, 1(4): 307-320.

Tertiary Education Commission. (2020). Targeted training and apprenticeship fund. https://www.tec.govt.nz/funding/funding-and-performance/funding/fund-finder/targeted-training-and-apprenticeship-fund/

Williamson, D. & Harris, C. (2019). Talent management and unions. *International Journal of Contemporary Hospitality Management*, 31(10), 3838-3854.

Wilson, M. (2004). The Employment Relations Act: a framework for a fairer way. In Rasmussen, E. (Ed.). *Employment relationships: New Zealand's Employment Relations Act* (pp. 9-20). Auckland University Press.

Wong, K., Chan, A.H.S & Ngan, S.C. (2019). The effect of long working hours and overtime on occupational health: A meta-analysis of evidence from 1998 to 2018, *International Journal of Environmental Research and Public Health*, 16(12), 2102.

About the authors

Erling Rasmussen is the Professor of Work and Employment at Auckland University of Technology (AUT). He has worked in employment relations for over 40 years and is currently involved in research projects on topics such as employment relations in the hospitality industry, conflict management and resolution, labour market adjustments and comparative employment relations. He has worked in the private sector in the United Kingdom and has been a government policy advisor in New Zealand. Erling has been an academic researcher in several OECD countries.

Felicity Lamm is currently an Associate Professor and the inaugural Co-Director of the Centre for Occupational Health and Safety Research at the Auckland University of Technology (AUT). In 2018, she was also appointed the Chief Advisor on Occupational Health and Safety for the New Zealand Government. She has been teaching and researching in the areas of employment relations and occupational health and safety (OHS) for over 30 years. She has written extensively on these subjects, including research reports for New Zealand and overseas public and private sector organisations. Over the years, Dr Lamm has been appointed to numerous governmental inquiries and advisory committees in New Zealand and internationally.

Julienne Molineaux (PhD) is a political scientist in the School of Social Science and Public Policy at Auckland University of Technology (AUT). She is a former executive member of the New Zealand Political Studies Association and former Director of The Policy Observatory. Julienne is currently an Associate Editor of the New Zealand Journal of Employment Relations. Her interest in employment relations focuses on politics and public policy, which she co-writes about for the Journal.

Gemma Piercy-Cameron (PhD) is a lecturer in Social Policy at the University of Waikato in Aotearoa New Zealand. Her research interests include: employment relations and tertiary/adult education and training, the role of unions, the changing nature of work, work identities and craft. She has published several articles and book chapters investigating the apprenticeship systems in New Zealand, Australia and Britain. Gemma is currently researching public policy transfer, new work identities and the post-2018 reform of New Zealand's vocational education and training system.

Michael Fletcher (PhD) is a Senior Research Fellow in the Institute for Governance and Policy Studies at Te Herenga Waka, Victoria University of Wellington. Prior to academic life, Michael worked for many years as a researcher, policy advisor and manager in various New Zealand government agencies, including the Department of Labour, the Families Commission and the Ministry for Social Development, working mostly on labour market and social policy topics. His current research interests centre around welfare policy, employment and family policies. In 2018-19 Michael was appointed as the independent advisor to the Welfare Expert Advisory Group. He is also the New Zealand Correspondent for the Max Planck Institute for Social Law and Social Policy in Munich, Germany.

Acknowledgements

The authors would like to thank the many students they have taught over the years. Their interest in the topic and numerous questions have made the authors examine again the many and changing facets of employment relations. The authors have also benefited from collaboration and input from colleagues within and outside Auckland University of Technology. A special thank you goes to those friends and colleagues who have been directly involved in specific parts of the book: Danaë Anderson, Paul Chalmers, Shivashni Priya Singh, and Ronny Tedestedt.

Erling Rasmussen, Felicity Lamm and Julienne Molineaux

March 2022